James VI & I: First King of Great Britain

A Tudor Times Insight

Tudor Times Insights

Tudor Times Insights collate articles from our website www.tudortimes.co.uk which is a repository for a wide variety of information about the Tudor and Stewart period 1485 – 1625. There you can find material on People, Places, Daily Life, Military & Warfare, Politics & Economics and Religion.

Titles in the Series

Profiles

Katherine Parr: Henry VIII's Sixth Queen

James IV: King of Scots

Lady Margaret Pole: Countess of Salisbury

Thomas Wolsey: Henry VIII's Cardinal

Thomas Cromwell: Henry VIII's Chief Minister

Marie of Guise: Regent of Scotland

James V: Scotland's Renaissance King

Lady Penelope Devereux: Sir Philip Sidney's Muse

Lady Katherine Grey: Tudor Prisoner

Sir William Cecil: Elizabeth I's Chief Minister

Lady Margaret Douglas: Countess of Lennox

Sir James Melville: Scottish Ambassador

Tudors & Stewarts 2015

Lady Margaret Beaufort: Tudor Matriarch

James, Earl of Moray: Regent of Scotland

Mary I: Queen of England

Jasper Tudor: Brother & Uncle of Kings

Katharine of Aragon: Henry VIII's First Wife

Honor Grenville: Lady Lisle

People

Who's Who in Wolf Hall

Who's Who in Britain's Bloody Crown

Politics & Economy

The Field of Cloth of Gold

Succession: The Tudor Problem

The Pilgrimage of Grace & Exeter Conspiracy

CONTENTS

Preface

James VI & I was the first monarch of both Scotland and England. His accession to the English throne began the long process of union. James' life was in many ways a lonely one – he never knew his parents, although he felt affection for his wife, they were not close, and he suffered numerous abduction and assassination attempts. Yet these vicissitudes did not sour him nor make him vindictive. Instead, he tried to reconcile competing religious views, unite his two kingdoms and make peace in place of war. Sadly, his efforts never achieved complete success.

James travelled extensively around the lowlands and eastern Scotland and even went to Denmark to rescue his ship-wrecked bride. Once in England, he undertook the usual royal progresses, which became an increasing financial burden on his subjects.

Although James is not one of the best known of British monarchs, during his reign the ultimate flourishing of Shakespeare, Ben Johnson and the architect Inigo Jones took place. James' obsession with witchcraft is one of the most difficult things for modern minds to comprehend, but it resulted in a wave of persecution – which he may have regretted in the end. James' greatest claim to fame however, is his sponsoring of the *King James Authorised Version of the Bible* – the best-selling book ever published in English.

The material was first published on www.tudortimes.co.uk

Family Tree

James VI & I
King of Scots, King of England

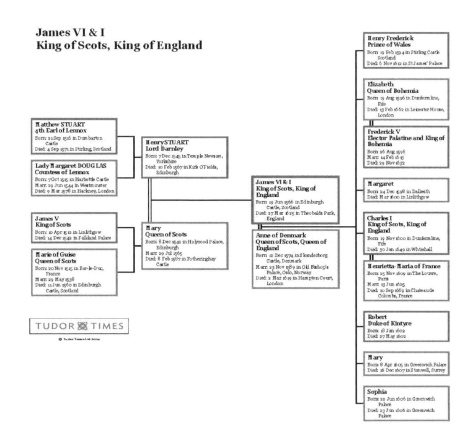

Henry Frederick
Prince of Wales
Born: 19 Feb 1594 in Stirling Castle, Scotland
Died: 6 Nov 1612 in St James' Palace

Elizabeth
Queen of Bohemia
Born: 19 Aug 1596 in Dunfermline, Fife
Died: 13 Feb 1662 in Leicester House, London

Frederick V
Elector Palatine and King of Bohemia
Born: 26 Aug 1596
Marr: 14 Feb 1613
Died: 29 Nov 1632

Matthew STUART
4th Earl of Lennox
Born: 21 Sep 1516 in Dumbarton Castle
Died: 4 Sep 1571 in Stirling, Scotland

Lady Margaret DOUGLAS
Countess of Lennox
Born: 7 Oct 1515 in Harbottle Castle
Marr: 29 Jun 1544 in Westminster
Died: 9 Mar 1576 in Hackney, London

Henry STUART
Lord Darnley
Born: 7 Dec 1545 in Temple Newsam, Yorkshire
Died: 10 Feb 1567 in Kirk O'Fields, Edinburgh

James VI & I
King of Scots, King of England
Born: 19 Jun 1566 in Edinburgh Castle, Scotland
Died: 27 Mar 1625 in Theobalds Park, England

Margaret
Born: 24 Dec 1598 in Dalkeith
Died: Mar 1600 in Linlithgow

Charles I
King of Scots, King of England
Born: 19 Nov 1600 in Dunfermline, Fife
Died: 30 Jan 1649 in Whitehall

James V
King of Scots
Born: 10 Apr 1512 in Linlithgow
Died: 14 Dec 1542 in Falkland Palace

Marie of Guise
Queen of Scots
Born: 20 Nov 1515 in Bar-le-Duc, France
Marr: 29 May 1538
Died: 11 Jun 1560 in Edinburgh Castle, Scotland

Mary
Queen of Scots
Born: 8 Dec 1542 in Holyrood Palace, Edinburgh
Marr: 29 Jul 1565
Died: 8 Feb 1587 in Fotheringhay Castle

Anne of Denmark
Queen of Scots, Queen of England
Born: 12 Dec 1574 in Skanderborg Castle, Denmark
Marr: 23 Nov 1589 in Old Bishop's Palace, Oslo, Norway
Died: 2 Mar 1619 in Hampton Court, London

Henrietta-Maria of France
Born: 25 Nov 1609 in The Louvre, Paris
Marr: 13 Jun 1625
Died: 10 Sep 1669 in Chateau de Colombs, France

Robert
Duke of Kintyre
Born: 18 Jan 1602
Died: 27 May 1602

Mary
Born: 8 Apr 1605 in Greenwich Palace
Died: 16 Dec 1607 in Stanwell, Surrey

Sophia
Born: 22 Jun 1606 in Greenwich Palace
Died: 23 Jun 1606 in Greenwich Palace

TUDOR ✖ TIMES
© Tudor Times Ltd 2024

Part 1: James VI & I's Life Story

Chapter 1: Christening to Coronation

It is the usual practice to begin a life story with a birth, but for James, an event which shaped his life completely occurred some two months before he was born.

On 9th March, 1566, his mother, Mary, Queen Regnant of Scotland, was having a private meal in her palace of Holyrood, with her half-sister, Jean, Countess of Argyll, various courtiers, and her secretary, an Italian by the name of David Riccio.

Into the midst of the dinner party erupted an armed band, led by the Queen's husband, Henry Stuart, once Lord Darnley, but given the title following his marriage, of King of Scots, the Earls of Ruthven and Morton and at least a dozen of their supporters.

The King held the Queen captive whilst Ruthven pointed a loaded pistol at her pregnant belly. Meanwhile, Riccio was dragged, screaming, from her presence, and stabbed over fifty times.

The aftermath of this assassination completely overturned Scottish politics. Mary, always quick-thinking and physically courageous, persuaded the King to desert his co-conspirators, and the two of them left Holyrood in secret. They rode for Dunbar, a distance of some thirty miles, which Mary, despite her advanced state of pregnancy, covered in around two hours.

Back in control, Mary banished the assassins, with the exception of her husband, who denied that he had known the plan was to kill Riccio, even though he had actually been the prime mover – instead, he blamed the others. He had deeply offended his wife by his original crime, and now he had betrayed his allies. He had signed his own death warrant.

In June, Mary, who had retired to the safety of Edinburgh Castle, gave birth. Surprisingly, considering the strain she had been under, the birth, although long and painful, resulted in a living child. The news was swiftly sent south to the English court, with Sir James Melville, and to Mary's French Guise family, and the Duchy of Savoy, whose Duke, Emmanuel Philibert, had promised to act as godfather. Services of Thanksgiving were held in St Giles' Kirk.

On 17th December, James was baptised, with a show of ceremony and splendour such as had not been seen in Scotland since the days of the baby's grandfather, James V. This was the only occasion during her personal rule when Mary raised taxation for expenditure outside the normal business of government – she was determined to show that her son was the legitimate heir to the crown of Scotland, and perhaps also to that of England.

In 1560, during Mary's absence in France, Protestantism had been instituted by the Estates of Scotland as the state religion. Mary had agreed to respect this, on the understanding that she herself would remain Catholic. The nobility, like the people, were divided between the old religion and the new, but the Protestant Lords, led by Mary's half-brother, Lord James Stewart, Earl of Moray, had the upper hand in government. They were not best pleased when Mary had James baptised in the Chapel Royal of Stirling with the full ceremonial of the Catholic church, presided over by the Archbishop of St Andrew's, with three assisting bishops, and the Catholic nobility of Scotland.

As well as the Duke of Savoy, the other godparents were Mary's brother-in-law, Charles IX of France; Elizabeth I of England, represented by the Earl of Bedford, and the Countess of Argyll. Elizabeth was Mary's cousin, and Mary had a strong claim to be, if not actually Queen of England (Elizabeth's legitimacy was questioned by many) then certainly her heir, under the usual laws of English inheritance.

Moray, who had once been in high favour with Queen Mary, until he objected to the marriage with Darnley, was present at Stirling, but refused to attend the ceremony, as did the powerful Earl of Bothwell. The baby's father, Darnley, although the Queen had expected his presence, and purchased a suit of cloth-of-gold, refused to engage in a ceremony in which he would not be recognised as king. Further controversy arose with the entertainment for the guests, including a masque which the English believed insulted them. The dancers were dressed as imps or devils and brandished their tails in such a way that the English took offence.

Chapter 2: Education

Soon after his birth, James was entrusted to the care of John, Earl of Mar, and his Countess, Annabella Murray. The little boy was to be kept safe at Stirling, as the politics of the Scottish court became increasingly fraught.

In February of 1567, the house where Darnley was recuperating from an illness, was blown up with gunpowder, and Darnley's body (unmarked by the explosion) was found in the garden. Immediately, suspicion fell on the Earl of Bothwell, but Mary, either believing him to be innocent, or, perhaps herself involved in the scheme (Mary's innocence or guilt has sparked controversy for five hundred years), seemed reluctant to pursue the investigation thoroughly. Not only that, she permitted Bothwell, following a swift trial at which he was acquitted, to carry her crown and sceptre at the state opening of Parliament.

Shortly after, she visited James at Stirling, but Mar refused to permit the baby to be taken out of Stirling – determined to safeguard the little prince. Events quickly unravelled for Mary, and she was forced to abdicate. James was crowned as King of Scotland on 29th July 1567 at the age of 13 months.

James' coronation was controversial – he was not immediately recognised as king by a significant proportion of Scots, let alone by foreign rulers. Even Protestant England was reluctant to involve itself with the deposition of a sovereign monarch. The ceremony, which took place in the Church of the Holy Rood (Holy Cross) in

Stirling, was as Protestant as his christening had been Catholic, with no less a luminary than John Knox preaching the sermon.

The Regency government that was formed consisted largely of those lords who had certainly slaughtered David Riccio, and may well have had a hand in Darnley's death. Chief amongst them was the Earl of Moray, instituted as regent, with the Earl of Morton as Chancellor. Morton read James' coronation oath on his behalf. The coronation over, James was returned to the care, first of the Earl of Mar, and, after Mar's death in 1572, to that of the earl's brother, Sir Alexander Erskine.

Lady Mar, described by John Knox as *'a sweet titbit for the Devil's mouth'* (which makes her sound rather more fun than Knox) was not an affectionate mother-substitute - James held her in *'great awe'*. However, such a role would not have been expected of her at the time. James' physical and emotional needs would have been provided by his wet-nurse and his intimate servants such as the four rockers.

It was important for his advisors that James be brought up without any taint of Catholicism. Two tutors were appointed – the first, George Buchanan, was a leading light of the Scottish Reformation and a man of great experience and ability. As well as having worked with Queen Mary on her Latin, he had, at one time, been teacher to no less a philosophical hero than the Frenchman Michel de Montaigne. Buchanan, who was well into his sixties when he became James' tutor, had very radical ideas on the role of kingship. He believed that the power and authority of the monarch was not unlimited, but subject to the will of the ruled.

Whilst Buchanan undoubtedly influenced James strongly – the young prince became a prodigy of learning and intellectual skill – he completely failed to instil any idea of the limitation of monarchical power. According to Sir James Melville, whose memoirs provided much of our knowledge of the period, Buchanan was somewhat cantankerous and unforgiving in his old age. On one occasion, having punished the king with a box on the ear, which led James to answer back, the boy was soundly beaten. The Countess of Mar chastised Buchanan for laying hands on the 'Lord's Anointed,' to which Buchanan replied that as he had 'whipped the King's arse', she could kiss it if she chose. James later recalled Buchanan with respect, admiration for his learning, and a healthy dose of remembered fear – telling a minister that his approach caused the king to tremble because it reminded James of his old teacher.

Fortunately for James, Buchanan's assistant was a much younger and more amenable character: Peter Young, who remained employed by James in various posts for many years, was more inclined to teaching by gentleness.

The result of James' education was a man who could read and write in Scots (a Germanic language, similar to, but not the same as English), Latin, French and Greek. He had studied history, philosophy and, most important in his tutors' eyes, his religion. The Scottish Reformation had been Calvinist in nature, more radical than the Protestant Reformation in England, which many Calvinists felt to be barely better than Roman Catholicism. James, whether by nature or training, had a prodigious memory, and knew most of the Bible by heart – which enabled him to have the last word in almost any argument for the rest of his life.

Chapter 3: Regents

It was not all book-learning. Like any young nobleman of the time, James learnt to ride, to hunt and to hawk with his school-room companions, chief of whom were the Earl of March's son, John Erskine and the Countess' nephew, John Murray. Perhaps surprisingly in view of our ideas about Calvinism, Buchanan also taught the young prince to dance, which he did *'with a very good grace,'* according to Melville. Despite this, James did not inherit any of the love or talent for music that his ancestors in both the Stewart and Tudor families had displayed.

Whilst James was being carefully educated, the world outside the safety of Stirling was a dangerous place. Scotland was riven between the *'Queen's Party'* which wanted to see Mary restored, and the *'King's Party'*, which actually held power. In 1570, Moray was assassinated. His place as regent was taken by James' grandfather, Matthew Stuart, Earl of Lennox. Lennox, although nominally Catholic, was supported by England – in part because his wife, Lady Margaret Douglas, was in England, and effectively hostage for Lennox' good behaviour.

Lennox had the distinction of being equally unpopular with the King's Party for his religion, and the Queen's Party for his antagonism towards her (he blamed her for his son, Darnley's, death). Before long, he too had fallen victim to violence, in a bloody raid on Stirling Castle in November 1571 that may have been intended as a kidnap attempt.

Lennox was succeeded by the Earl of Mar, who died within the year. His death may well have been from natural causes, but poisoning was suspected, administered on the orders of none other than the Earl of Morton, who now took over as regent in November 1572. Morton had been one of Riccio's murderers, but, paradoxically, this ruthless man eventually brought the civil war to an end by vanquishing the Queen's Party at last. James was still only five years old and had lost two regents to violence and a third to disease. Morton imposed a semblance of peace, but was much resented by many of the nobles, particularly the Catholic Earls of Argyll and Atholl, and James' new guardian, Sir Alexander Erskine, who had taken that role after Mar's death. Morton was strongly supported by the English government, morally if not financially.

Morton also had little support from the Kirk, which felt he lent towards an Episcopal model of church government, rather than the Presbyterian model they wished to follow. Matters came to a head in March 1578, when James was not quite twelve. Argyll and Atholl informed the king that they wanted the other nobles to arbitrate a quarrel they had with the regent. Morton responded that if Argyll and Atholl were not punished, he would be forced to resign as regent. The earls and Erskine immediately seized on this and advised James to accept the resignation and proclaim himself as at the head of government. This was duly done, and on 8th

March, James took his place in Council for the first time. Whilst Morton was forced to retreat from the public eye and surrender control of Edinburgh Castle, Holyrood, and the Great Seal, necessary for public business, he was permitted to retire to Lochleven, where he apparently enjoyed a brief holiday gardening. Within weeks, though, Morton had regained control of Stirling, in a raid in which Erskine's son was killed, to the grief of both himself and James.

Morton now once again controlled the person of the king. Whilst he had strong support from England, with James now adolescent, a new model of government had to be found, and Parliament was called to make suitable arrangements.

Morton was reinstated as President of the Council, although not as regent, and the membership was broadened to include Atholl, who soon died, following a banquet with Morton. Rumours of poison became persistent, and eventually a post mortem was held, which concluded that Atholl had died of natural causes. During this last flurry of power, Morton's old enemies in the Queen's Party, the Hamiltons, were finally crushed.

This unsettling year had a profound effect on James – the loss of Erskine's son, the midnight attack at Stirling and the violence gave him nightmares. The English envoy, Sir Robert Bowes, recorded that *'his Grace by night hath been so discouraged as in his sleep he is therefore greatly disquieted.'*

Chapter 4: Coming of Age

James had had a sniff of control, and, as he reached his thirteenth birthday in summer 1579, he began to flex his muscles.

He left Stirling that autumn and made his first formal entry into his capital city of Edinburgh. The day was an occasion of spectacle and pageantry – tableaux of Scotland's kings, and of Solomon granting wise judgement, greeted him. The city dwellers were treated to free wine and, probably less popularly, Latin speeches. At his side was the man whom James had turned to as an antidote to the odious Morton – Esmé Stuart, Sieur d'Aubigny. Esmé was from the branch of the Stuart family that had settled in France during the fifteenth century, and served the French crown as soldiers and diplomats. He was also first cousin to James' father, Lord Darnley.

At the age of 37, Esmé was too old to be James' friend in the usual sense, but before long the young king became completely devoted to him. Described as charming, and by the Catholic Bishop of Ross as 'comely', and of 'marked prudence', he was also, having been brought up in France, Catholic. This fact alone would have led to disapproval from the Kirk, but the ministers were also upset by his 'great ruffes' and 'side bellows (exaggerated trunk hose)'. There has been much speculation about whether James' relationship with this much older man was what we might nowadays call 'inappropriate', but given that the child had been starved of any real affection or parental love, it is not hard to conceive that his hero-worship of his glamorous cousin might have been quite innocent of any sexual element.

Morton felt his influence waning, as Esme was granted the earldom of Lennox (his elderly uncle, the previous earl, was persuaded to accept the title of Earl of March in exchange). He also succeeded to the offices traditionally held by the Lennoxes, including custody of the great fortress of Dumbarton Castle.

Following the entry into Edinburgh, James had declared to the Estates that he was of age to govern himself, and dismissed Morton to retirement. The English were alarmed at this turn of events – their picked man had been forced out of office, to be replaced by a French Catholic. Lennox' conversion to Calvinism in May 1580 was seen as a cynical move to gain power. His enemies probably wronged him in this, as he remained true to the Protestant faith for the rest of his life. In a vain effort to restore Morton and English influence, a plot was allegedly hatched, with Elizabeth and her minister, Burghley's, connivance, to kidnap James and assassinate Lennox. More openly, Elizabeth hinted to James that he might be chosen as her heir – but that consorting with French Catholics was not the way to clinch the matter.

Whether the plot really existed in any meaningful way, is moot. Morton was thoroughly disliked, and not just by James. Lennox is credited (if such be the word) with the plan that eventually dispatched him. On 1st January 1581, one of Lennox' adherents, Captain James Stewart (whose sister, Margaret was John Knox' widow) burst into the Privy Council chamber and denounced Morton as one of the murderers of Lord Darnley. Morton vehemently denied the charge, but was arrested and taken to Dumbarton. He was brought back to Edinburgh for trial on 1st June, at which he admitted having been an accessory before the fact, but insisted that Bothwell had been the prime mover. He was found guilty. James refused to read his letters, although he did commute the sentence of hanging, drawing and quartering to something swifter, and the earl was executed by an early prototype of the guillotine.

Shortly after, Lennox' earldom was raised to a dukedom (the only one in Scotland not conferred on a prince of the royal family) and Captain Stuart became Earl of Arran, in place of the Hamilton earl, who had been insane for many years. For the next few years, Lennox and Arran were chief amongst James' advisors.

Chapter 5: James and the Kirk

Although Lennox' conversion to Calvinism appears to have been genuine, he was no friend to the notion that the Kirk should have equal, or even more authority, than the king. If James had had any doubts as to what the Kirk expected of him, he could consult the book by his old tutor George Buchanan, *De Jure Regni Apud Scotos* which very clearly declared that king ought to be the servant of his people.

It is paradoxical to note that the Protestant Reformation which had so vehemently argued against Papal and Ecclesiastical power should emphasise the authority of the Kirk – although it was democratic in that the members appointed the leaders. This idea of the Kirk's authority was outlined in the *Second Book of Discipline*, first published in 1578, which claimed that although the king was supreme in civil matters, *'all godly princes and magistrates'* ought to be guided by the Kirk.

This was certainly not the sort of idea that kings, even so young as James, liked to entertain and he rapidly became a supporter of the traditional church hierarchy which included bishops. At first glance it may be difficult for those of us not involved in the arcane complexities of church government in the 16th century to understand the difference between the superintendents of the Kirk and the bishops of the traditional church. The distinction lies in the belief that the superintendents ought to be selected by, and ultimately answerable to, the godly church members of the congregations, rather than being part of a separate priesthood. For James it was important that bishops be seen as representing authority that derived from the king's appointment rather than from the people.

Doctrinally, James never wavered from his Calvinist upbringing. In 1581, to clarify his religious position, a document called the *'King's Confession'*, or sometimes the *'Negative Confession'* was drawn for signature by both king and people. In it the signatories confirmed their allegiance to *'the true religion'*, their opposition to the Roman Catholic Church and their willingness to defend the king, the gospel and the country. The document was drawn up by John Craig, the Moderator of the

General Assembly (the governing body of the Kirk) who had once been a Dominican friar, until converted by the doctrines of Calvin.

Despite his genuine support for the Protestant Kirk, James was very ready to accept the principles of regal and ecclesiastical hierarchy that Lennox espoused, whose experience of life in France gave him a more exalted view of the powers of kingship. The advent of Lennox also introduced James to a wider cultural media, particularly the pleasures of poetry, promoting a circle at court which became known as the Castalians, who wrote in Scots. James himself frequently wrote poetry, but it was never more than competent.

Lennox' arrival also led to a rapprochement with the deposed Mary. During his childhood James had heard nothing but ill of his mother. Buchanan, having once been full of praise for his queen, had denounced her in the worst terms as an adulteress, murderess and idolater. James now began to reassess these ideas and to equate criticism of Mary with the undermining of royal authority. In 1584 the Estates formally condemned Buchanan's writings.

Such a rehabilitation of Mary's reputation did not, of course, mean that James was prepared to give up his throne in favour of his mother. Lennox had come to Scotland to achieve the Guise mission of restoring Mary either completely, or in joint authority with James, with James ruling in fact. Whilst many of the old Queen's Party, such as Maitland of Lethington and Lords Seton and Maxwell, favoured the scheme, for many it was seen as the slippery slope towards a return to Rome and was vehemently opposed. James was, to begin with, keen – it would legitimise his sovereignty in the eyes of Catholic Europe and give their joint weight to their claim to the English throne. Soon however, it dawned on James, perhaps with the help of another of his new favourites, Sir Patrick Gray, that such a scheme would actually place obstacles in his way to power at home and in England. He corresponded with his mother, whilst at the same time advocating that the Association should only take effect on the basis that she would remain confined in England.

Chapter 6: The Ruthven Raid

James had begun the policy which was to continue for his whole life, of appearing to agree with all sides and then finally doing what he had always intended. He listened to the Spanish and French envoys, took into consideration the pros and cons of extending the scheme of rapprochement to enforcing his and his mother's claims to the throne of England by invasion, and eventually decided that his best course of action was to maintain his adherence to the Protestant church and win the English throne via a positive relationship with Elizabeth.

As he entered his adolescence, James began to deviate somewhat from the behaviour expected of the godly Calvinist Prince. Unlike his mother's cousin, Edward VI, who as king from the age of nine, became more and more devoted to his Protestant religion and concentrated much of his energy on religious matters, James began to take a more relaxed approach, sometimes missing services and spending more time in his favourite occupations of hunting and hawking. Unlike previous generations of royal princes, there does not seem to have been much of a military element to James's education although he enjoyed the sport of running at the ring – a game of skill in which the rider had to approach at full speed the target of a ring suspended from a crossbeam and thrust a lance through it.

With James's lack of interest in the idea of joint sovereignty with Mary, and his growing maturity and desire to look at every possible angle of the situation, his relationship with Lennox began to cool. At the same time Lennox and his friend, Arran, quarrelled. According to Sir James Melville, Lennox was a good and well-meaning man, given poor advice and betrayed by self-seeking friends who envied his position with the king. He was also the subject of plots by those who wished to take power into their own hands. Stedall, in his book 'The Survival of the Crown' sees Lennox as a master plotter, whose complex machinations led to his own undoing.

In time-honoured fashion, the unhappy Scots nobles decided that kidnapping the king would be the answer to their problems. They therefore took advantage of a hunting trip that James was making, whilst Lennox and Arran were both away from court. Melville recounts that he received a visitor, who wished to remain nameless, who warned him that there was a plot to kidnap the king. Melville, not entirely believing the story, went to Lennox at Dalkeith where the duke was holding a justice in Ayre. Melville recommended that Lennox should ride immediately to the king's side, but Lennox, not knowing that one of the conspirators was the

Earl of Gowrie, sent a message to that earl, presumably thinking that that would be the best way to protect the king.

Instead, in a variation to the original plot now required because Lennox had been warned, the next day, 22nd of August 1582, Gowrie intercepted the king's hunting party and invited him to visit Gowrie's castle at Ruthven.

James apparently suspected something was amiss but as he only had a small party he was not able to resist. He took the decision to go to Ruthven, believing that he could escape easily the next day under pretext of another hunting trip. Meanwhile, Lennox had sent a message to Arran to come as quickly as possible, whilst he himself rode as fast as he could towards James. Being informed that James had already been captured, Lennox took refuge in Dumbarton. James himself was carried off to Stirling and Arran was also captured.

Throughout the autumn of 1582, James was so closely guarded it was impossible for Lennox to affect any kind of rescue. Queen Elizabeth and Charles XII of France both gave the impression of being shocked at this kidnap of an anointed monarch and sent messages of support. James, either playing a longer game or terrified of his captors, assured the foreign ambassadors that he was perfectly content with his advisers and he concurred with their opinion that their actions had been of service to himself and to the country. He sent similar messages to the General Assembly. The lords then prevailed upon James, with scarcely veiled threats, to dismiss Lennox. At length Lennox realised that there was no prospect of him being united with his friend and he returned to

France as commanded. James had been compelled to write to Lennox in angry terms, accusing him of disloyalty and inconstancy. In response Lennox wrote to James assuring him of his fidelity and obedience and that it was James whom *alone in this world [his] heart [was] resolved to serve.'*

Lennox died in early 1583, declaring his constancy to the Protestant church and requesting that his heart be sent to James.

Chapter 7: Escape

Despite James' ability to dissemble in front of the lords who held him captive, Melville notes that he took the matter very much to heart, he felt not just grief for the loss of his friend but also shame in front of other monarchs for his seeming powerlessness and anger that his lords should treat an anointed king with such little respect.

But as often happens with lords who kidnapped kings in the 15th and 16th centuries, they found themselves hoist with their own petard. They had to make a convincing show that they were acting in the king and country's best interests and they needed the king's authorisation for any acts they undertook. There was also the expense of maintaining His Majesty, and the money that they had been promised from England was not forthcoming in the kinds of quantities they had hoped.

Beginning to understand that James might not be so easily controlled as they had hoped, Gowrie and his colleagues retired from court to indicate that they had no intention of trying to control him. James, who had perhaps lulled them into a false sense of security by a show of compliant behaviour for several months, seized his opportunity and secretly sent messages to many of the nobility to convene at St Andrews. He did not include any of the lords who had abducted him in the summons.

Amongst those summoned by James were the earls of Huntly, Argyll, Montrose, Crawford, Rothes and March. He also requested the presence of Melville who, whilst complaining about being brought out of retirement, advised James that the best course of action that he could take on now attaining his majority, and full control of the country, would be to forgive and forget any past misdeeds.

James, who was at Falkland Palace, then informed his attendants that he would ride to St Andrews as he had received an invitation to dine from the Earl of March. Whilst these attendants, who were of course in position because of their support of James's abduction, protested and suggested that he ought to wait for Gowrie and his colleagues, James insisted, and they did not dare to prevent him leaving.

As soon as he was at St Andrew's, it became apparent that James meant to take control. Accounts differ as to the role of Gowrie at this point – Melville claims that James summoned him personally, believing that the earl was penitent for his role in the abduction. Other sources suggest that Gowrie was hurrying towards St Andrews in the hope of keeping the king under his control. Whichever is the truth, it was soon apparent to Gowrie that James would never be under his influence again. He fell to his knees and begged forgiveness. James graciously replied that the Raid of Ruthven would be forgiven.

James declared to his assembled nobles that he was now king in fact as well as in name. He was 17 years old and intended to rule impartially and bring them all to *'unity and concord'*.

The English ambassador, Sir Robert Bowes, was disappointed that James would keep all his personal papers himself and that there was little opportunity for getting hold of them.

James was not temperamentally suited to the day-to-day business of government. He was of a strategic, rather than a tactical, turn of mind. He could, at least in his own opinion, transact more business in an hour than other men could do in a day and could simultaneously write, think, listen and give orders. He therefore delegated a good deal of routine business to the Earl of Arran, a proceeding which was as unpopular as such actions often are – more through the envy of those who were not chosen than the belief that the king should do everything himself. Arran himself was also personally unpopular and associated in many people's minds with the pro-French, pro-Catholic policy that Lennox had been accused of. Sir James Melville is certainly scathing in his assessment of Arran as the underlying cause of the Ruthven Raid and a likely exacerbation to faction.

Whether it was Arran's doing or James' own long-term plan is debatable, but in May 1584 Gowrie was accused of a new act of treason and executed. Not only Gowrie but also the earls of Angus and Mar were disgraced and forced into exile in England. This led Elizabeth to write a rather sententious letter admonishing James for having broken his word to forgive the Ruthven Raid. The reality was, of course, that the English were always happy to promote dissent Scottish court.

Chapter 8: Early Foreign Policy

James was also determined to stamp his authority over the Kirk, whose most vociferous defender was Andrew Melville, who had taken on Knox's mantle as Scotland's premier religious radical and was Moderator of the General Assembly. Once free of the Ruthven lords, James was determined that there would be no more nonsense (as he saw it) about the king and the civil government being required to take the advice and guidance of the Kirk.

In 1584 parliament passed what became known as the Black Acts. Under this legislation, the presbyteries were condemned and the king was acknowledged as having supreme power over the church, together with the right to call General Assemblies.

In a further show of independence, James entered into correspondence with his Guise relatives and also wrote to the kings of France and Spain and, in surprisingly polite terms, to the Pope. Presumably irritated by Elizabeth's interference, he was sounding out the possibility of foreign support against his tiresome neighbour. James also talked expansively about his support for his mother, whom he claimed was wrongly imprisoned and whom he would always support.

Simultaneously he was assuring Elizabeth's ambassador, Sir Robert Bowes, that Mary's Catholicism made her unfit to rule in either Scotland or England. The French soon became aware that his support for Mary did not go so far as wishing for her return to his own detriment. In some ways this accorded with their own views – despite regular complaints from France, Spain and the Pope about Mary's treatment there was never any real intention to take meaningful action against Elizabeth.

Whilst Arran was still James's chief Minister, he also had a new confidant, Sir Patrick Gray. Gray had once been a confidential servant of Mary's but he had become convinced that there was no hope for her and that his best interests lay with promoting an agreement between James and Elizabeth. In 1584 Gray was commissioned to go to the English court with proposals for an alliance. He was in a prime position to share Mary's innermost secrets with Elizabeth and her ministers.

Gray obviously proved persuasive, or else the declining relationship with Spain caused by Elizabeth's somewhat reluctant support of Philip II's Protestant rebels in the Netherlands made an agreement with James highly desirable. Elizabeth agreed to pay the impecunious king a pension of £4000 per annum. This was undoubtedly a practical decision for James, as the Act of Association that had been pushed through the English Parliament by the factions most hostile to Mary enacted that anyone who benefited from an act of assassination against Elizabeth would be automatically debarred from the throne even if they had had no hand in it. Thus any plot to free Mary and put him on the throne would automatically negate James's rights. Although had Mary actually become Queen this Act would have been rapidly overturned the reality was, that by 1584 Mary's chances of a successful coup were fading.

Mary, deeply hurt by this defection of her son, attempted to disinherit him and name Philip II as successor to her rights to the English crown – not quite so far-fetched as it sounds as Philip had a good dose of Lancastrian blood.

As Gray became more important in James's counsels, Arran's influence with the king began to wane. Scenting blood, his many enemies sought to strike. An ideal opportunity occurred when Francis Russell, the son of the Earl of Bedford, Elizabeth's Lieutenant in the North, was killed in a border raid on one of the regular truce days. The offender was Sir Thomas Ferniehurst, one of Arran's appointees. There is no evidence at all that Arran was involved, however it became convenient to hold him responsible. James, concerned by the prospect of the loss of the English alliance, passed some 24 hours in deep distress, before ordering his Chancellor's arrest. After a week, James gave orders for his release, but shortly afterwards the exiled earls of Angus and Mar, together with those others involved in the Raid of Ruthven who had been kicking their heels in England, marched on Stirling Castle with sufficient troops to persuade James that it was time for

Arran to retire. He was stripped of the chancellorship and sent into obscurity.

James now pardoned the former exiles but felt no obligation to be as accommodating to the Kirk, especially when the lords showed little enthusiasm for the radicalism of Andrew Melville and his colleague, John Gibson. Melville was encouraged to travel to the Highlands to try to root out Jesuit priests whilst Gibson was informed by the king that he '[gave] not a turd for [his] preaching' and sent to prison for criticising James's maintenance of bishops within the church as 'tyranny'.

With Arran in retirement, the chancellorship was granted to John Maitland, a brother of Maitland of Lethington who had been Mary's secretary. James' Council was now composed of a wide range of his nobles from all factions. This, together with his pension from England, although it was not paid with any great regularity, made him more secure on his throne than he had ever been.

Chapter 9: The Execution of Mary

In 1586, James was faced with a moral dilemma, although his power to actually act was limited. Sir Francis Walsingham, one of the chief members of Elizabeth's Privy Council, and an inveterate enemy of James's mother, had, through a combination of entrapment, espionage and daring, uncovered (or created) the

Babington plot, to assassinate Elizabeth and put Mary on the throne of England.

It was evident that, if Mary had not actually approved the assassination of Elizabeth, she was well aware that it was planned. This information was used to condemn her for treason. James, not surprisingly, was completely unable to believe that Elizabeth really intended for Mary to be executed. Indeed, Elizabeth herself found it difficult to bring such a momentous event to pass.

James wrote a number of letters begging that Mary's life be saved, but at the same time he knew that the Act of Association would render any pleas he made for Mary, fodder for any those sought to exclude him from the English succession.

Having deposed their queen some 20 years before, the nobles and commons of Scotland now affected to be horrified at the idea that a foreign government might take it upon itself to execute her. Under pressure to show that Scotland was a sovereign country, and that James was of equal standing with Elizabeth, the king wrote his cousin a letter which caused Elizabeth to explode in fury. In it, he pointed out that her father's execution of her mother, Anne Boleyn, had not been so heinous a crime as her execution of a fellow sovereign would be.

Once she had been persuaded to calm down enough to respond, Elizabeth replied to this missive with the statement that his letter meant that she would not now intervene to delay any proceedings against Mary: a handy way of passing the blame for Mary's death to James. In addition, she refused to receive any delegation from

Scotland led by nobles, requiring that any embassy should be led by commoners.

Nevertheless, it was clear to the English that James would do no more than protest. The Earl of Leicester was assured that alliance with England was a key component of James's policy, from which he would not deviate unless absolutely forced to do so. It was obvious that the only thing that might force James to take more aggressive note towards his southern neighbour would be a definite decision on Elizabeth's part to name a different successor.

James knew that to break with England could only be politically feasible if he were to ally with Catholic Spain. It was an open secret that Philip II was planning an invasion of England but his success was by no means guaranteed and a policy of alliance with a Catholic nation would be highly unpopular with the majority of James' nobles. He could therefore do no more than plead for Mary's life, and pledge that she would, if spared, take no part in any further conspiracies. He assured Elizabeth that her life was no less dear to him than his mother's, and that he was constant in his friendship towards her country.

James accepted that there was nothing he could do to help Mary. The English government, with or without Elizabeth's heartfelt consent, was determined to make an end of her and she had given them the means to do so. James, a committed Protestant whose overriding ambition was to inherit the Crown of England and who had little or no power to challenge England, was obliged to swallow the bitter pill.

There are mixed reports of how James received the news of his mother's death – some suggesting that he was glad that he was now truly king at last, another suggesting that he was upset and depressed. We must remember that James could not possibly have remembered Mary, whom he had not seen since he was 10 months old.

James was very pleased to accept Elizabeth's protestations that the actual execution had nothing to do with her, but that her secretary William Davidson had exceeded his authority by sending the warrant for execution.

Chapter 10: The Armada

James's reluctance to become too closely allied with Spain proved the wiser course. With Mary dead, Philip was far more interested in conquering England to make it one of the dominions of his own family, specifically to see his daughter, the Infanta Isabella Clara Eugenia, crowned, rather than Protestant James. It was perfectly apparent to James and his subjects that if Spain were to conquer England, Scotland wouldn't be far behind. In the view of some of James's Catholic nobles, such as Huntly, Crawford and Montrose, this was not necessarily a bad thing. Whilst they did not want a Spanish monarch, they did wish to see James convert to the old faith.

James was fond of Huntly and was also willing to encourage a certain level of Catholicism to act as a counterbalance to England. James himself, although firmly Protestant, and indeed a denouncer of '*Papism*', was not of a mind to persecute others for their religion. Indeed, he was so confident of his own religious beliefs that he challenged Huntly's Jesuit uncle to a public debate in which even the Spanish ambassador had to admit he showed himself as master of his subject. A certain discreet encouragement of Catholics would also stand him in good stead with those Englishmen (and they were legion, although declining in numbers) who hankered after the old ways.

When he was finally put to the test in the summer of 1588, James confirmed his alliance with England and offered no aid to Spain either through helping any of the ships of the Armada that were wrecked on his coasts or by causing disturbances in the borders. Elizabeth does not appear to have been particularly grateful for his abstinence and despite promises, he received little material reward.

Whilst the king might have refrained from any support for Spain, he was put in an embarrassing position when the English government produced letters, apparently written from the Earl of Huntly and others, to Philip, bemoaning the failure of the '*Enterprise of England*' and suggesting that the Duke of Parma should land 6000 troops in order to begin a joint invasion of England.

With little choice but to take some action, James had Huntly arrested and imprisoned in Edinburgh Castle. The imprisonment was hardly severe, as James dined with the earl, but took the opportunity to reprove him for his actions, having believed that Huntly's signing of the King's Confession (see above) a few months before had shown evidence of the genuine conversion. Huntly was released but rearrested when Chancellor Maitland threatened to resign. The earl was sent to his northern estates, but James was unable to condemn him wholeheartedly.

Before long, it seemed that this leniency might have been a dire error. Huntly, together with the earls of Bothwell, Errol and Crawford, who all had a grievance over the influence of Maitland, advanced on Edinburgh, apparently with the resolve of subjecting James to abduction yet again. Warned of the attempt, James took refuge in Maitland's house, and the earls found themselves foiled. Even James felt that his former friend had gone too far, and he raised an army which marched swiftly on Aberdeen, the seat of Huntly's power. Declining to fight, Huntly's men evaporated and the earl himself, promised clemency, gave himself up as did his confederates, Crawford and Bothwell. The earls were convicted of treason but following a short, and not unduly rigorous, confinement, were released, much to the disgust of the Kirk and Queen Elizabeth, who had both hoped to see Catholic influence in Scotland crushed.

Chapter 11: Marriage Negotiations

In 1589 James turned 22, and it was time for him to marry. A number of brides had been proposed at different times - the two leading candidates were the Huguenot Catherine of Navarre, whose brother Henri was fighting to take possession of the throne of France (favoured by England), and Anne of Denmark, a Lutheran Princess, and distant cousin of James'. As Catherine's prospects seemed uncertain in the wake of her brother's struggles to claim his French throne, Anne seemed a better candidate, especially as her rival was some eight years older than James and rumoured to be less prepossessing physically than Anne.

Negotiations for Anne's hand had begun in 1587, under the aegis of the king's former tutor, Peter Young, but matters had stalled when agreement over the dowry could not be reached. James was initially inclined to the elder daughter of the King of Denmark but was perfectly happy to settle for Anne when it appeared that Elizabeth was already spoken for.

In early 1589, James's envoy, George Keith, Earl Marischal, sailed to Denmark to negotiate in earnest. The Scottish list of demands was eye watering – a dowry of £1 million Scots, confirmation that Denmark would give up its claims to the Orkney Islands (transferred to Scotland when Christian I had been unable to pay the dowry of his daughter Margaret, wife of James III of Scotland). Denmark was also to agree to be part of any anti-

Catholic alliance and to support James militarily if he were faced with invasion or, (and this was the tricky bit), had to fight for any foreign title to which he was justly entitled. Denmark was therefore agreeing, in principle, to an invasion of England, were such a course to prove necessary to obtain the crown. Anne's father, Frederick II, having died in 1588, the prime mover for the marriage was her mother Sophia of Mecklenburg-Güstrow, a woman of formidable character.

James had persuaded himself that he was romantically in love with his new bride and pressed for the marriage to go ahead. Queen Sophia, who had already invested an enormous amount of money in Anne's new wardrobe, which had taken several months of work from 500 tailors and embroiderers, did not wish to see her good work undone. Eventually, a compromise was reached on the dowry which was eventually settled at 75,000 thalers, which assuming them to be equal to the Imperial thaler, was equal to about £150,000 Scots.

This decision to accept a bride without a large dowry did not help James' permanently impoverished position. He had absolutely no grasp of finance and spent money he did not have – not so much on himself, as in generous gifts. Feeling the pinch, he was obliged to borrow money from Elizabeth for his wedding.

The couple were married by proxy in Copenhagen on 9th September 1589 and 15-year-old Anne duly set out for her new home three weeks later. She had no sooner set sail than terrible storms beset her flotilla. The seas were so rough that three canon escaped their moorings on her flagship, the *Gideon*, and careened around the deck. Three times the ships were forced back into port. The captain of the ship, Peter Munk, blamed witchcraft for the dreadful tempests. He believed that he had been cursed by the wife of a man with whom he had quarrelled.

By 8th October James was seriously alarmed as to the whereabouts of his new bride. He sent letters and love poems by the messenger whom he dispatched to gather information as to her whereabouts. It was not until 10th October that he was informed that the Princess was safe, but had been obliged to take shelter in Oslo.

In one of the few romantic gestures of his life, James determined to sail to fetch his bride himself. Borrowing the necessary money from Maitland, James confided his affairs to a Privy Council composed of members of all the factions under the nominal presidency of Ludovic Stewart, the 15-year-old Duke of Lennox, son of James's old friend Esmé Stuart. This was a perfectly proper selection as Lennox was James's heir, although the Earl of Bothwell felt himself slighted.

Chapter 12: Wedding

James set out with a contingent of six ships and arrived in Oslo in November. He immediately raced to see his young bride and attempted to steal a kiss from her at their first meeting, which somewhat embarrassed the young lady. Within a couple of weeks they had been married at St Halvard's Church in Oslo and their marriage got off onto a good foot with both of them appearing to be happy to follow the convention that married couples should love each other. Although over time they did not prove to be particularly well-suited, in the main they rubbed along pretty well, despite some questions about James's fondness for his male favourites. Anne bore seven children, the first in 1594 and the last in 1606 although only three survived infancy, of whom the eldest, Henry Frederick, died at eighteen.

James' honeymoon trip was something of a holiday. He remained at the court of his young brother-in-law, Christian IV, until late April 1590, entertaining and being entertained in both the traditional fashion of drinking and feasting but also in intellectual pursuits, such as religious debates, a discussion about demonology with a Lutheran theologian, Hemmingius , an introduction to Copernican theory and meetings with the famous astronomer, Tycho Brahe. James was given a silver goblet in commemoration of a three-hour speech which he delivered in Latin to the University of Copenhagen.

After James and Anne had witnessed the marriage of her sister, Elizabeth, to the Duke of Brunswick, the Royal couple departed, landing at Leith on 1st May. The new Queen of Scots make a formal entry into Edinburgh on 6th May in her silver carriage drawn by eight white horses. On 17th May she was crowned as queen in Holyrood Abbey. There had been fierce objections by the Kirk about the use of oil to anoint her during the ceremony – this being traduced as papist superstition. James overrode their objection by pointing out the frequency with which biblical kings had been anointed with oil and suggested that if the General Moderator of the Assembly, Robert Bruce, did not wish to perform the ceremony he was sure that one of the bishops could be prevailed upon to do so. No further complaints were made!

Chapter 13: Witchcraft

The difficulties Anne's fleet had experienced had been attributed to witchcraft, and an unhealthy interest in the topic was now spreading through Europe. During the Middle Ages, whilst the Catholic Church was quite confident in the existence of the devil, the official line was that witchcraft was a nonsensical delusion inculcated by the devil to entrap people into pagan errors. Persecution had been almost non-existent prior to 1400.

In the late 15th century, witchcraft began to be taken far more seriously with the publication of the *Malleus Maleficarum,* a treatise written by the German Dominican friar, Heinrich Kramer. By the latter half of the 16th century the prevalence of persecution of witches had increased dramatically across Europe. In 1537, Janet, Lady Glamis, had been accused of endeavouring to bring about the death of James V by witchcraft and burnt. James, despite his huge intellect and wide-ranging education, had no doubt in the 1590s of the existence of witches and witchcraft.

Whilst we may take any belief in witchcraft with a healthy dose of scepticism, people believed in it, and some even practised it, in the sense that they would cast spells, however efficacious or not they might have been. Several members of the Scottish nobility were believed to be involved with witchcraft: in particular, Margaret Fleming, who was the grand-daughter of James IV and her great-grandson, Francis, Earl of Bothwell, who was also first cousin to James VI (via an illegitimate son of James V).

Bothwell was a member of the king's Privy Council. He had urged on James the necessity for making war on England after the execution of Mary, Queen of Scots, but James had ignored his advice. Bothwell, like most of James' nobles, had spent a brief time 'warded' (effectively under house arrest) in Edinburgh Castle for various misdemeanours. But by mid-1587 was back at court, and appointed Lord High Admiral, with responsibility for protecting Scotland against any encroachment by the Spanish Armada that was anticipated would be sent against England.

In 1590-91 the most notorious witch trial of James' reign began in North Berwick. During the interrogation and torture of dozens of women and some men, some admitted to sorcery, and Bothwell was named as the leader of the coven. He was arrested in April 1591. Over the following three years, Bothwell was imprisoned, pardoned, ordered into exile, released, broke into James' bedroom causing the king to fear both assassination and the loss of his soul, attainted and finally exiled in a bewildering confusion of events.

James continued to believe in demonic practices, and in 1597 published his 'Daemonolgie' a treatise in which he used Biblical verses extensively to prove the existence of witches. During his reign in England, anti-witchcraft measures were strengthened, and there were dozens of accusations and perhaps some 300 deaths in total between Scotland and England during James' reign. Two particularly noteworthy incidents being the 1612 Pendle witch trials, and the curious case in 1613 surrounding the Duke of Rutland, described in Dr Tracy Borman's book, '*Witches*'. The persecution, although horrible, was not on anything like the scale in continental Europe where tens of thousands died. By the end of his life, James began to doubt, not the wiles of Satan, but rather the methods used to extract confessions, and his enthusiasm for the topic waned.

Chapter 14: Treason and Murder

During the 1590s, James had to deal with several nobles who were fomenting rebellion, treason, and assassination, as well as witchcraft. The ringleaders of the various plots were the Earl of Huntly and the Earl of Bothwell.

Following James' forgiveness of Huntly mentioned above, he, together with his confederate, Errol, had continued to correspond with Spain. Not content with this, he arranged the murder of the Earl of Moray (son-in-law of the Regent Moray). Moray was a Protestant and extremely popular – '*the bonny Earl of Moray*' - although not with James, who disliked him. There were also rumours that Queen Anne was fonder of Moray than she ought to have been, which, in the first flush of marriage, James might have resented.

Huntly and Moray had been feuding for years (no doubt in part because of the history of their fathers covered in the Tudor Times Insight *'James, Earl of Moray: Regent of Scotland'*). James decided that he would try to reconcile the two and Moray was invited to Dunbirsle Castle in Fife. Before any attempt at reconciliation could be made (if that were James' real intention), Huntly had left the king's hunting party, on the excuse that he was searching for associates of the outlawed Earl of Bothwell, and set fire to Dunbirsle with Moray and his men inside. With the flames raging all around him, Moray ran out of the castle to the shore, where he was butchered by Huntly and his men. It was widely believed that James had been party to the plot.

Huntley gave himself up, amidst cries for vengeance from Moray's mother, the Kirk and the Protestant party. James again showed a level of leniency that was wholly out of keeping with his duty as a monarch and brought down rebukes from Queen Elizabeth, who pointed out that no good could come of petting Catholics.

Meanwhile, Bothwell was at large, and as a Protestant, he was championed by the Kirk, although his association with witchcraft and his general propensity to lawlessness gave him the character, in the words of one minister, of *'a sanctified plague'*, sent to keep James on the path of Protestantism.

The murder of Moray, who was Bothwell's cousin, did not discourage Bothwell from treasonable acts. He made an attack on Falkland Palace where James and Anne were staying and was only beaten off after a seven-hour siege. The next time, James was not so lucky.   On 24th July, 1593, Bothwell broke into the royal bedchamber.   Fearing for his life, James agreed to pardon all Bothwell's crimes, including the charges of witchcraft, for which he had been condemned.   For the next few months, James had the humiliation of being surrounded by Bothwell's men (the earl himself agreed to withdraw from court) whilst he pretended that all was well.

In due course however, James managed, yet again, to persuade the moderate nobles to support him, and he escaped from Bothwell's clutches.   Bothwell continued to make trouble, but when an assault on Edinburgh was defeated, his support from England ceased.   James appeared to have the upper hand, until Bothwell, in a surprising volte-face that lost him the support of the Kirk, joined forces with Huntly, who together with the Errol, Angus and Sir Patrick Gordon, were currently under investigation for what became known as the 'treason of the Spanish blanks.'   A series of blank sheets of paper with the signatures of the said earls were found in the possession of a messenger heading for Spain. The inference was that they were giving consent to some plot requiring Spanish support.

James again failed to take immediate decisive action, but by late 1594 the disobedience of the Catholic earls and Bothwell had risen to such a pitch that he had no alternative but to raise troops and seek to crush them once and for all.   The northern fastnesses of Huntly, Errol and other Catholics in the Highlands were destroyed and the earls driven into exile.   Bothwell died in 1612 in Naples, but Huntly and Errol were permitted to return on condition that they signed the Protestant Confession of Faith and entered the Kirk. They did so, but it was only lip service – in 1636, Huntly died a Catholic.

Nevertheless, James was now back in control of affairs so far as rebellious nobles were concerned. He also sought to strengthen his standing with the Kirk. Government by presbyteries within the Kirk had finally been conceded, and the 1584 Act which enshrined the position of bishops, was repealed. James also gave some succour to English Puritans who had been fleeing persecution south of the border. This put his relationship with Elizabeth at some risk, but she did not want to drive him too far into the waiting arms of Spain - which his willingness to overlook the Spanish blanks made possible – so she did no more than fume at him.

Chapter 15: Taming Scotland

By 1595, James was 29 years old. He had survived kidnaps, assassination attempts, armed conflict and, in his own eyes, witchcraft. He now had a son (Prince Henry Frederick) to succeed him, and from this point onward, he would brook no further disobedience. According to a proclamation published in that year '..he will be obeyed and reverenced as a king, and will execute his power and authority against [anyone]'.

James had relied heavily on Maitland as his chancellor. Maitland, a servant of the state in a similar mould to Sir William

Cecil south of the border, had been unpopular, seen as usurping the rights of James' nobles to order the government. Following his death, a group of eight ministers undertook most of the administration – all from the ranks of the lower nobility, and initially charged with improving the miserable royal finances. James was so broke that he wrote one day that the kitchen staff had run away and refused to cook supper, because their wages had not been paid.

Whilst retrenchment was effective for a short period, the good work was not kept up and James fell into deeper and deeper debt.

Further troubles arose when it became apparent that Queen Anne, brought up as a Lutheran, had become, not a good Calvinist, as might have been hoped by the Kirk, but a secret Catholic. She was denounced publicly by David Black, minister of St Andrew's in October 1596 and when James remonstrated with him, Black insisted that, when in his pulpit, he was subject only to God. James, seething, bided his time, but eventually achieved his aims. In December 1596, following riots stirred up by radical ministers in Edinburgh outside the Tolbooth where James was meeting with the Lords of Session, the king declared that he, the queen and the whole court would no longer be resident in Edinburgh, as it was not fit to house a king.

Horrified at the idea of the loss of trade that this would bring, the more moderate burghers of the city distanced themselves from the firebrands and offered the king their apologies and paid a handsome fine without complaint.

The General Assembly of the Kirk agreed to send representatives to Parliament, to show that it accepted temporal control by the king. These representatives, who were to be drawn from the best-educated ministers were to be called 'bishop': they were quite different, James claimed, from Catholic or Anglican bishops, but the principles of hierarchy and of ecclesiastical submission to the crown, at least in political terms, had been established. Three new bishops were created by James, to join the Kirk in parliament, although they had no authority within the Kirk.

James also made some progress on taming the lawlessness of the border country between Scotland and England, which had been a thorn in the side of both countries for generations. His careful courting of Elizabeth was helpful here as it resulted in the setting up of an Anglo-Scottish Commission to deal with the problem in 1597, which it did with some success.

During these years of relative peace, James spent more time writing, and amongst other things, produced the work *Basilikon Doron*, a treatise written for his son, Henry Frederick, on the duties and art of kingship.

Chapter 16: The Gowrie Conspiracy

Into this haven of peace erupted another scene of violence, the truth behind which has been argued over for centuries. In summary, James was at the house of the Earl of Gowrie and his brother, Lord Ruthven. In a private room with Ruthven, James cried out 'treason'. One of his attendants, Ramsay, entered the chamber to find James in a struggle with Lord Ruthven. Ramsay killed Ruthven, and in the ensuing mayhem as all of James' attendants and Gowrie raced to the scene, Gowrie too was killed. The Ruthven brothers were accused of treason, as were their younger brothers who had been absent, found guilty and subject to the forfeiture of their lands. Their bodies were hanged and quartered, and the heads placed on the Mercat Cross.

These are the bald facts, but at the time, and ever since, it has been wondered whether James set out to murder the Ruthvens in revenge either for their father's murder of David Riccio back in 1566, or for the kidnapping of James himself (see chapter 6). Certainly the king's account of the matter sounded far-fetched and inconsistent, but, as he pointed out himself, if he wanted the Ruthvens dead, there were far less risky methods he could have chosen and he certainly had no personal history of violent action. Besides, Ruthven was considered to be a favourite of the king, and his sister, Beatrice, was one of Queen Anne's favourite attendants.

On the other hand, it is difficult to imagine that if Ruthven really wanted to kill James that he would have been overpowered by the king, and in any event, a murder of the king would have been unlikely to have passed without comment by the population – surely the Ruthvens would have been caught and hanged?

James made good use of the events – with the Gowrie lands forfeited, his £80,000 debt was also nullified. He also ordered public thanksgivings and recalcitrant members of the Kirk who seemed to have believed that James had planned the whole thing, were replaced with more malleable ministers.

A very detailed explanation of the plot and the possible interpretations may be found here. http://www.online-literature.com/andrew_lang/historical-mysteries/7/

Chapter 17: Across the Border

As the sixteenth century drew to a close, James became increasingly impatient to be officially recognised by Elizabeth as her heir, an action she refused to take. He did not necessarily help his cause by giving tacit support to the Earl of Tyrone, whose Irish uprising would embroil the English crown for some ten years. Although James made proclamations against his subjects giving Tyrone assistance, he failed to back up his words with gestures.

He was also making overtures to both the Puritan and the Catholic parties. He informed the Puritans that he would 'maintain the profession of the gospel' and not permit any other religion (than Protestantism) to be professed throughout the kingdom. At the same time, he was assuring the Catholic party that so long as Catholics maintained outward conformity to the law, he would not trouble them, and would, indeed, reward those who deserved it. These two statements can be made compatible, but only with a certain elasticity of interpretation – a thing in which James excelled!

There was a faction at Elizabeth's court in the 1590s that was tired of the queen, the dominance of Burghley and his son, Sir Robert Cecil, and eager for change. They began to correspond with James. Chief of these were Robert Devereux, Earl of Essex, and his sister, Lady Penelope Rich, nee Devereux. James was rather non-committal in his responses to their overtures, and when Essex was finally executed for treason in 1601, James instructed his ambassadors to request Elizabeth to publicly exonerate James from any involvement. Naturally, Elizabeth declined to make any such statement.

With Elizabeth's life obviously drawing to a close and his enemy, Essex, dead, Sir Robert Cecil began a correspondence with James in which he promised to smooth the way for James' inheritance, a day which he claimed to hope was very far off. The third party to their secret correspondence was Lord Henry Howard, whose brother, Thomas, 4th Duke of Norfolk, had been executed for conspiring to marry James' mother. Assured of the support of the most influential minister in England, James waited more patiently for his turn. Cecil took the opportunity of the growing trust of James to undermine Elizabeth's other favourite, Sir Walter Raleigh.

On 24th March 1603, Elizabeth breathed her last at Richmond Palace. The legend is that within moments, one of her ladies had dropped a ring out of the queen's bedroom window to the waiting horseman, Sir Robert Carey, who made all speed for Scotland and arrived in record time, late on the evening of the second day. The reality is a little more complex – whilst Carey had the ring, he did not set out for Edinburgh until he had been assured that the Privy Council intended to proclaim James as king.

James set out from Holyrood on 5th April 1603. Queen Anne was pregnant, so she remained behind, as did the royal children. It was planned that Anne, Henry Frederick and Elizabeth would follow the king shortly, whilst the little Prince Charles, who was not robust, would remain in Scotland for the time being.

On his last Sunday in Edinburgh, James made a speech to the congregation in St Giles Kirk, Edinburgh, in which he assured the Scots that they would lose nothing by his accession to the English throne – that he intended to establish peace and concord between the two nations and increase the prosperity of both. He would return, he promised, every three years - in the event, he returned only once, in 1617.

For the Scots, there was mingled pride that their king was now King of England, Ireland (tenuously) and France (in fantasy) and fear lest they be abandoned. There seemed little doubt that he would move south permanently, and that, after the anticipated reign of Henry Frederick, there would be no more kings born in Scotland. On the plus side, the costs of war, both human and monetary, would be likely to decrease, and trade might improve – although England's chilly relations with France and Spain might not help that hope.

As he travelled south, James was met by swathes of courtiers, hoping to win favour early. In particular, the Catholics of the north hoped that tolerance would soon be the order of the day. However, as de Lisle points out in *'After Elizabeth'* whilst James might favour individual Catholics, Catholicism per se was just as unpalatable to him as it had been to Elizabeth in her later years.

Chapter 18: Union of the Crowns

James quickly made it plain that he wanted his Privy Council to comprise both English and Scots. The introduction of Scots, and the king's desire to extend *'denization'* (effectively citizenship) to all Scots in England, was a bit of a shock to Sir Robert Cecil, who had retained his place, and his colleagues, but they had little choice but acceptance. They were also somewhat disgruntled by his command to have Elizabeth's jewels and clothes sent to Anne, protesting that the items should not be sent out of the country. James insisted that some be sent to her, although he mollified them by saying that he did not mean state jewellery to be sent so far away.

Anne and the older children joined the king in early summer, in time for king and queen to be crowned together. Owing to an extremely virulent outbreak of plague, the coronation was a low-key affair – not improved by Anne's refusal to take Communion in the manner prescribed by the Anglican Church.

Whilst the factional politics of the English court were far less likely to break out into open violence than in Scotland, nevertheless, there were bitter feuds and James, if he had been in doubt of their existence before his accession, soon became aware of them. He sought to heal one old wound by releasing the Earl of Southampton from the Tower, where he had been languishing since Essex' Rebellion of 1600. Although Cecil and Essex had been at loggerheads, and James was content for Cecil to be his Secretary, he spoke of Essex as his 'martyr', and he and Anne showed remarkable favour to Essex' sister, Lady Penelope Rich, at least until she alienated the king by marrying against Church command. James also showed favour to those who had supported his mother.

James now sought to promote peace and unity on a larger scale – between his two, or rather, three (including Ireland) realms. One of his earliest acts was to proclaim Scots money as legal tender in England. Another was to order new coinage with the symbols of both nations.

In his first English Parliament of 1604, he declared his intention to oversee a wholesale union between the countries:

'What God hath conjoined let no man separate. I am the husband and the whole isle is my lawful wife; I am the head and it is my body; I am the shepherd and it is my flock. I hope therefore that no man will think that I, a Christian King under the Gospel, should be a polygamist and husband to two wives.'

Nevertheless, he could not persuade either the English or the Scots to give more than 'consideration' to the matter. In particular, the English parliament objected to the notion that Scots should have equal rights in England. There were concerns that a tide of 'hungry Scots' would wash its way over England. The point was eventually decided by the famous 'Calvin's Case 1608', in which it was held by a majority of fourteen that Scots born after the king's accession to the English throne had the same rights as Englishmen. Those born prior to 25th March 1603, remained 'aliens.'

By 1605, it was reported by the Venetian Ambassador that 'the question of the Union will, I am assured, be dropped; for His Majesty is now well aware that nothing can be effected, both sides displaying such obstinacy that an accommodation is impossible; and so his Majesty is resolved to abandon the question for the present, in hope that time may consume the ill-humours.'

Nevertheless, by Royal Proclamation, James changed his title and that of his successors, to King of Great Britain. He also sported two new coats of arms, with the 1st and 4th quarters the Lion of Scotland when north of the border, and the English lions and lilies 1st and 4th in England. The Union flag, which was introduced (minus the Ulster saltire) gained little currency.

For the first few years, there was a good deal of disquiet, as many of James' personal friends and servants, not surprisingly, were Scots and the king's generosity – or rather prodigality, for he gave gifts and grants he could not afford – was resented. Over time, however, the English courtiers accepted that James was genuine in his desire to have both English and Scottish advisers and moderated their complaints.

During James' years as King of Scots, he had cultivated good relationships with the Protestant countries of Europe – some of the German states and Scandinavia. The old Franco-Scottish alliance had worn thin (Henri IV was opposed to his succession to the English crown as it would remove France's age-old strategy of keeping an enemy on England's doorstep) but had endured. He was even on relatively good terms with Spain, although his moral, if not financial, support for the Netherlandish Protestant insurgents was not appreciated by the Spanish.

As King of England, he inherited an ongoing war with Spain, and a bloody and terrible war in Ireland that was dragging to a horrible conclusion with the final defeat of the Irish earl, Hugh O'Neill by Lord Mountjoy – rewarded by James with the earldom of Devonshire. Following the increased control of Ireland, the policy of Anglo-Scottish *plantations* in the country, which had begun under Henry VIII, continued.

James immediately sought peace with Spain by withdrawing the *letters of marque* from private vessels. A letter of marque was effectively a licence to prey on enemy shipping, although it frequently was no more than an excuse for outright piracy. The Treaty of London, bringing some twenty years of hostility with Spain to an end, was signed in 1604. James also ceased official support for the Netherlands, although, unlike the Spanish, they were still permitted to recruit in England amongst their fellow Protestants.

Chapter 19: The Puritans & Hampton Court Conference

On James' accession, there was the mainstream Anglican established Church – ruled by the Act of Uniformity of 1559, which mandated the use of the Book of Common Prayer 1552, with minor amendments, supported by the 1571 Subscription Act which required observance of the Thirty-Nine Articles of the English Church. Theologically, the Articles were a mixture of Catholic and Calvinist teaching, intended to allow the widest possible spectrum of people to accept the Church.

As with many compromise positions both sides felt aggrieved and throughout Elizabeth's reign competing forces of Catholicism and puritanism sought to capture the English Church.

A section of the Anglican clergy wanted it to be further purified of '*Romish*' practices, such as Confirmation, wedding rings and ecclesiastical vestments. These were the moderate Puritans, not really comparable with the Presbyterians who had given James so much trouble in Scotland, as they did not support the radical sects who wanted to reform Church government root and branch.

During his progress from Edinburgh to London, a delegation of these Puritans had presented James with a petition, known as the '*Millenary*' petition because it had received over 1000 signatures. James had responded positively to the petition, he assured the clergy that he would promote the Word of God and not permit any other religion to flourish in his kingdom. Before long, James' Council and the mainstream clergy had convinced him that the Puritans were the equivalent of the Scottish Presbyterians who had caused him so much trouble, and that their aim was to create an ecclesiastical order that was not subject to the king's authority.

Given that the position of the Puritans was doctrinally the same as the mainstream Church, James believed that he could affect reconciliation over the '*indifferent*' matters. He therefore called a conference at Hampton Court to take place in January 1604 in which four leading ministers from the Puritan wing: Dr Reynolds, President of Corpus Christi College, Oxford; Laurence Chaderton, Master of Emmanuel College, Cambridge; Thomas Sparks and John Knewstubs, were permitted to bring forward their arguments. These four were by no means radicals, and had close relationships with the bishops, although the latter two had been involved in the Presbyterian movement.

The mainstream clergy were led by John Whitgift, Archbishop of Canterbury, and eight bishops. The conference made some concessions to the Puritans, mainly in areas where abuse was obvious: Church discipline was to be improved, with legal experts to support bishops in Church courts; better observation of the Sabbath was to be enforced; baptism was to be undertaken only by ministers, although it could be carried out in private homes if necessary; abolition of pluralism was stressed again, as was the need for well-educated ministers to teach their flocks. Unfortunately, the bonanza of the dispersal of Church lands during the mid-sixteenth century meant that there was little money to pay an educated clergy.

It was also agreed that a new translation of the Bible should be commissioned, which was published in 1611 and is known as the

King James' Authorised Version – cornerstone of the traditional Anglican Church.

The Conference was completed at the end of four days. Although it had achieved some of its aims, the principle one of reconciling the Puritan element with the Church was not fulfilled. All clergy had to comply with the Book of Common Prayer, and the rules on vestments by November 1604 or leave the Church. Nor had the views of the more radical Puritans been taken into account. Although there were no major disputes between James and the Puritans during the rest of his reign, trouble would flare up under his successor.

Chapter 20: The Catholics and the Gunpowder Plot

At the same time as mollifying the Puritans, James had tacitly let it be assumed by Catholics that he would allow the practice of their religion. He had no inclination towards religious persecution *'...[I will] never agree that any should die for an error in faith'* and during the period prior to his accession he was in close contact with the Earl of Northumberland, who, although nominally Protestant, was certainly a Catholic sympathiser. The new king likewise welcomed Lord Henry Howard, brother of the late Duke of Norfolk, and a suspected Catholic, to his Privy Council and soon granted him the earldom of Northampton. There was also the Catholic Earl of Worcester and Northampton's cousin, Lord

Thomas Howard, soon to be Earl of Suffolk. Suffolk, and more particularly his wife, were known as Catholic sympathisers.

There was also the matter of Queen Anne's religion. At some point, she seems to have converted to Catholicism, and in the early days of the English reign, was eager for Prince Henry Frederick to marry a Catholic. Initially, James relaxed the recusancy laws, and intimated that he would turn a blind eye to Catholics who worshipped privately. Before long, the numbers of Catholics who ceased attending Church was so great that James assumed that wholesale conversions were taking place, rather than that Catholics were pouring out of hiding. Alarmed, he back-tracked and became absolutely insistent that the law requiring Catholic priests to leave the country should be rigorously enforced.

The Catholic faction was divided: on one hand were the secular priests who were content to live under James and swear allegiance to him as king, on the other were the Jesuits who wanted to overturn the Protestant succession and sought nothing less than the unravelling of the Reformation. These two parties were at daggers drawn and on a number of occasions betrayed each other. In particular, an early plot, known as the Bye Plot, which centred on the idea of kidnapping James in 1603, was betrayed by the Jesuits (although the specifics are rather more complex). The Bye plot was related to another, marginally more feasible plot, termed the Main Plot.

The Main Plot centred on the replacement of James with his cousin, Lady Arbella Stuart. The government alleged that it was concocted by Henry Brooke, 12th Lord Cobham (brother-in-law of

Cecil), and was funded by the Spanish government – although why the Spanish government would prefer the Protestant Arbella to the Protestant, but generally sympathetic James, was never made clear. Sir Walter Raleigh (against whom James had been strongly influenced by Cecil, Northampton and Suffolk) was accused of involvement – although, again, why such a notorious enemy of Spain should involve himself in such a plot was not explained very satisfactorily. Leanda de Lisle in her book 'After Elizabeth' discusses the ins and outs of the Main Plot in detail. One result of the plot was the long-term imprisonment of Raleigh, who remained in the Tower for thirteen years.

The most famous of all the Catholic plots, and the one that had the most damaging effect on public perceptions of Catholicism for four hundred years after it occurred, was the Powder Treason, as it was known – now called the Gunpowder Plot.

The plot was led by Robert Catesby, who had been fined for recusancy on numerous occasions. Catesby was a member of a circle of Northamptonshire gentry that included the Treshams, Vaux, and Throckmortons in a web of intermarriage. In 1601, he had been involved in the Essex Rebellion, for which he was fined 4,000 marks (about £2,600).

The plot itself was brilliant in its simplicity – to blow up Parliament with the king, the Prince of Wales and the Duke of York inside, and to replace them with the Princess Elizabeth, who would be a puppet queen for a Catholic government. Planning the plot took some time and effort – a house was rented with cellars from which the cellars under Westminster could be reached, gunpowder was brought in, and tunnels dug.

Over time, more and more conspirators had to be drawn in. One of them, possibly, although not certainly, Sir Francis Tresham, was uncomfortable with the idea that Catholic as well as Protestant members of the Parliament would be killed. Tresham's brother-in-law, Lord Monteagle, received a letter warning him to stay away. It has been postulated that Monteagle wrote the letter himself to reveal the plot and gain favour.

Monteagle took the letter to James and Cecil (now Earl of Salisbury). The cellars were searched, and a man subsequently named, after extensive torture, as Guy Fawkes, was found with the gunpowder. Despite fleeing London, the majority of the conspirators were found (including Thomas Percy, brother of the Earl of Northumberland), tried and executed at the end of January 1606. Northumberland was sent to the Tower, where he remained for seventeen years and was fined £30,000.

James himself, whilst he maintained that the plot was the work of a few, and was not the responsibility of the many loyal Catholics in the country, became determined to force Catholics to choose sides. In 1606, the Oath of Allegiance was published. Catholics were required to swear that, so far as temporal matters were concerned, the Pope had no power to overthrow kings or to interfere in political matters outside his own temporal state. Many Catholics believed this, but the Oath led to controversy both at home and in Europe. James was not the only king who wanted to eradicate Papal interference in secular matters.

A full account of the plot may be read in Jessie Childs' *'God's Traitors'*. For the rest of James' reign, he continued to tolerate individual Catholics amongst his friends, ministers and court, but public advocacy, failure to conform to the laws or attempts to convert Protestants were punished with all the rigour of the law.

Chapter 21: The Rise of Robert Carr

It was widely known that James enjoyed the company of young men to a degree that certainly raised a few eyebrows in his own time, although the exact nature of his relationships cannot, of course, be ascertained. He had seven children by his wife, and whilst it was never a great romance, he remained fond of her until her death in 1619. Nevertheless, it was apparent that he did not have a close emotional or intellectual bond with his Queen, and did not, in general, have a high opinion of women – hardly unusual in a misogynist age. From around 1607, by which time the Queen had had several miscarriages and lost two children in infancy, they seemed to have stopped sleeping together. Anne was 33 and James was 41.

This increased distance from Anne seems to have revived James' early inclination towards male companionship. After his early close relationship with Lennox (see Chapter 4) there were other favourites, including Sir James Hay, and Philip Herbert, Earl of Montgomerie, but none that touched the king as did Robert Carr.

In 1607, Carr (or Kerr, as it was spelt in Scots), was twenty-one years old, son of Sir Thomas Kerr of Ferniehurst, Scottish Warden of the Middle March. He had spent some time in France, and was described by Sir John Harington (Elizabeth I's god-son, the inventor of the water-closet) as *'straight-limbed, well-favoured, strong-shouldered and smooth-faced.'*

Carr's first appearance at court came in March 1607 when, in attendance on Sir James Hay at a tournament, he was thrown by his horse and broke a leg. James insisted that he be tended by the royal physicians and took a personal interest in Carr's recovery. He visited frequently, and quickly came to dote on the young man. He began to teach his protégé Latin, and to spend a good deal of time with him.

Once Carr was recovered, James appointed him as a Gentleman of the Bedchamber, and walked around the court, leaning on the younger man's arm – a great sign of James' personal favour. Over the next three years, Carr was showered with grants and favours, attracting the disgust not only of the court but of Queen Anne and Prince Henry.

The latter's disapproval was silenced by his sudden death, aged eighteen, in November 1612. Although the relationship between the king and his heir had become tense, owing to Henry's support for Sir Walter Raleigh, his strident Protestantism, and general popularity, it was a terrible personal blow to both James and Anne.

Memory of his son's disapproval did nothing to cool James' affection for Carr, who by 1613 was Earl of Somerset and Lord Chamberlain.

Over the next few years, as Salisbury's influenced waned – mainly because he was fighting a rear-guard action to contain James' spendthrift habits which were leaving the Crown enormously indebted and in need of Parliamentary support for funding – Somerset's mastery grew. Somerset himself was not personally disliked – he was of a pleasant disposition, devoted to James, and not inclined to factionalism – yet his influence and his control of preferment was profoundly resented.

Eventually, Somerset could not stand aloof from court faction – on the one side, Northampton, Suffolk and the other Howards, and on the other, his own oldest friend, Sir Thomas Overbury, who aligned with a reforming group in Parliament. Matters came to a head when Somerset fell deeply in love with Lady Frances Devereux (née Howard), wife of the Earl of Essex, and daughter of the Earl of Suffolk. The Essexes had been married aged 13 and 14, but had not consummated their union. Apparently, the earl, no matter how often he bedded with his wife, could not summon up the necessary enthusiasm to perform.

By 1613, Somerset was Frances' lover, and the two hoped for an annulment of the Essex marriage, so they could marry. Overbury counselled Somerset strongly against it, criticising Frances as a 'base woman'. The Howards, of course, were keen for the marriage to take place.

James himself wanted Somerset to have his way and interfered unduly with the Ecclesiastical Commission set up to judge whether the Essex marriage could be annulled. In due course, Frances was free, but she and her family deeply resented Overbury's interference, and she arranged his murder.

Somerset had been shown so much favour by James that he began to be careless about pleasing his royal master, and by August 1614, a new young man was being talked of as very much in the king's eye – George Villiers.

Whilst Somerset might have faded gently into the background, the discovery in 1615 that Overbury had been murdered, led to a trial in which both Somerset and his wife were found guilty. She was pardoned but they both remained in the Tower for seven years. He adamantly refused to admit to any involvement. In 1622 they were released from prison, and in 1624 Somerset received a pardon. He lived more or less in obscurity until his death in 1645.

Chapter 22: The Duke of Buckingham

With Somerset out of favour, George Villiers now shot to stardom, rising from the fourth son of a country gentleman to being the only non-royal duke in either kingdom by 1623 as Duke of Buckingham. There are more indications that James and Villiers had a sexual relationship than is evident for any other of

James' favourites, although the passionate language used by men and women to friends of the same sex in the 17th century render it possible that despite what appear to be love-letters, the relationship might not have been consummated. Buckingham himself, whatever he might have done with James, was happy to engage in heterosexual activity, and to marry allegedly the richest woman in the country, Lady Katherine Manners, daughter and heir of the Earl of Rutland. Queen Anne was also fond of Buckingham and was glad to see him supplant Somerset, whom she hated.

The closing seven years of James' reign were controlled largely by Buckingham who worked closely with Sir Francis Bacon, who became Lord Chancellor in 1618. Between them, Buckingham and Bacon controlled a government that was becoming increasingly corrupt and divorced from James' earlier pronouncements on a king's duty to rule within the law (even though he was possessed of Divine Right).

James' reign had been a byword for financial corruption, prodigious overspending and blatant sale of offices by the Howard faction under Suffolk, Northampton, and, following his marriage to Suffolk's daughter, Frances, Somerset. Various retrenchment schemes had come to nothing in the face of royal extravagance and ministerial greed. James had introduced new revenue raising schemes, based on new or increased customs duties, known as impositions. He also hoped to obtain some much-needed cash through a dowry to be received for Prince Henry's marriage, but the prince's death had stymied that plan.

By 1614, James had no choice but to call Parliament for *'supply'* as taxes for government were (and, officially, still are) known, but the Privy Council was either not prepared, or was not able, to manage the Commons as Elizabeth had. James opened the session with the ambition that it become known as *'the Parliament of Love'* as he hoped to smooth away strife. But to no avail: within weeks there was deadlock as the Commons requested the Lords to join them in seeking to have the new impositions removed. The Lords refused, scenting sedition. The Commons therefore declined to consider the matter of supply.

James dissolved the assembly, and, far from it being the Parliament of Love, it is remembered as the Addled Parliament. But this still left him without money. Under Buckingham, although he took sweeteners for promotion to office, he was reasonably even-handed with whom he favoured, government made some strides towards getting the royal finances under control.

But this was not enough, and James continued to dream of a fat dowry for his son. Negotiations were opened with Spain, who promised an infanta with £600,000. In return, Catholics were not only to be tolerated, but were to be allowed to worship in the infanta's own Chapel Royal. Whilst there was no possibility that the English public would stomach such an arrangement, of which James was perfectly well aware, he continued to play along.

Meanwhile, responding to anti-Spanish feeling at home, he freed Sir Walter Raleigh with a view to the great seaman undertaking a voyage to South America that would, hopefully, result in discovery of a goldmine – or at least, the discovery of Spanish ships carrying the precious metal. The Spanish ambassador was assured that Raleigh's liberty was not an affront to his kingdom, and that if Raleigh interfered with a single Spaniard, he would pay for it with his life.

Unsurprisingly, the expedition fell foul of the Spanish, and Raleigh, on his eventual return was tried, convicted and executed. Even Queen Anne's plea for mercy, delivered via Buckingham, was rejected. For James, peace with Spain was more important than any other consideration.

But peace was not easily had – the clouds of religious war were again gathering over Europe. James' daughter, Elizabeth, had been married in 1613 to Frederick, the Elector Palatine. Before his death, the Catholic Holy Emperor Matthias, who was also King of Bohemia, had sought to have the elective Bohemian crown passed to his cousin, Archduke Ferdinand. The Bohemians were divided, but a breakaway group offered the throne to Elector Frederick.

James was appalled – he knew that Frederick could not accept the Bohemian throne without bloodshed, but he prevaricated. He sought to mediate between the two sides, but did not firmly tell Frederick and Elizabeth that they would not have his support. In the inevitable defeat of Frederick, James refused to engage with troops – he would not embroil his subjects in a needless war. Once again, in seeking to please everyone, he pleased no-one. Eventually, a small private force was raised to help Frederick re-establish himself in the Palatine, but it failed. The Thirty Years' War, the most destructive European conflict before the twentieth century was unleashed, killing between 5 and 11 million of the European population as Catholics and Protestants struggled for the continent's soul.

Chapter 23: The Last Years of James

With Europe descending into war, James, although still desperate to maintain peace, summoned Parliament once again. He sought a subsidy that would allow him to send forces to the Protestant armies, but Parliament was unimpressed with his continued courting of Spain, and voted only £145,000 rather than the £500,000 requested. In return, the Commons flexed their muscles with the impeachment of Sir France Bacon.

They also demanded that Prince Charles should be married to *'one of our own religion'*, rather than a Spanish bride.

Foreign policy was a matter for the government, not Parliament (as is still, theoretically, the case today). James was furious at the Commons' temerity in seeking to dictate policy, and he threatened to punish offenders. The Commons, provoked by this attack on their right of free-speech, drew up a *'Protestation'*, which was presented to James on 18th December 1621. James responded by immediately adjourning the house till the following February and tore the Protestation from the Commons' Journal. He also ordered the imprisonment of Sir Edward Coke, the Lord Chief Justice, who had been its principal author.

Insanity now seemed to be springing up at the English court –
Buckingham and Prince Charles cooked up a scheme for Charles to
cross-war torn Europe to court his Spanish bride in person.
James, at first resistant, was talked into approving the plan,
hopeful that the match would result in the return of the Palatinate
to Frederick and Elizabeth, and the two men left in disguise, to
appear in Madrid in March 1623. The next months saw the men
dancing attendance on the Spanish court and given negotiation
terms that were nothing less than outrageous. The Infanta was
not only to be allowed to practise her religion, her children were to
be brought up in it, and all penal laws against Catholics relaxed.

All this was agreed to, although Charles adamantly refused to
change his own faith, but then the Spanish demands went too far.
They wanted the Elector's oldest son to be married to the
Emperor's daughter and brought up a Catholic. It was obvious
that there had never been any intention on Spain's part to release
the Palatinate from their grasp.

Outraged, Charles and Buckingham combined to persuade
James to break off negotiations, and to call Parliament to vote
supplies for armed intervention in the Palatinate. Eventually,
James did so, and the final Parliament of his reign was
considerably more amicable. Funds for war were voted (to be paid
into a special treasury, to prevent leakage to courtiers), the
Commons' demands for the reduction of monopolies were
accepted and the Lord Treasurer, a supporter of the Spanish
match, was impeached and dismissed from office. James' own
financial position was not remedied, but, before further business
could be contracted the king died.

He had been ailing for some time, and it was probably a stroke, aggravated by malaria, that carried him off, although there was the usual talk of poisoning.

Conclusion

James VI & I was a man of huge intellect and lofty ideals. His aims throughout his life were entirely laudable – peace at home and abroad, reconciliation in religion (he even advocated a General Council of the Church) and good government at home. Unfortunately, his personal characteristics of trying to please everyone, being rather shifty about the truth, having an inflated view of his own brilliance and ability to convince others, and, most dangerous of all in a king, his lack of resolution to follow a policy through, meant that his reign was not so successful as it might have been. Nevertheless, he brought England and Scotland together in peace, promoted a church that the majority of his subjects could accept, and left an adult male heir – more than many of his predecessors had achieved.

Part 2: Aspects of James VI & I's Life

Chapter 24: Following the Footsteps of James VI & I

James travelled fairly extensively around the central and eastern parts of Scotland, and, once he became King of England visited a number of towns and great houses as part of regular progresses. He also undertook one voyage abroad, visiting Denmark in 1589 to fetch his bride. Many of the locations James lived in can be visited, although the buildings are not always visible.

The numbers in the article below correspond to those on the map which follows.

*

One of the events which had the greatest influence on James' life occurred before he was born in the Palace of Holyroodhouse, Edinburgh (1). His mother, Mary, Queen of Scots, heavily pregnant with James, was held immobile by her husband, Henry, Lord Darnley (also known as Henry, King of Scots) whilst her secretary, David Riccio, was assassinated in the next room. This incident would have a profound effect on the politics of Scotland, and James' own life. Today, the Palace of Holyroodhouse is the official home of the monarch as Queen of Scots. The chamber where Riccio was murdered can still be seen, along with treasures such as the Lennox Jewel, which James' grandmother, Lady Margaret Douglas, commissioned.

Queen Mary, ever resourceful, evaded the plotters, and persuading her husband to betray them, fled the capital for safety at Dunbar. She returned to give birth to James in the safety of Edinburgh Castle (2). The castle still stands today, towering over the city of Edinburgh, and home to the Honours of Scotland (the Crown, Sceptre and Sword) with which James was crowned at the age of thirteen months. The coronation took place, not in Edinburgh, but in the more easily protected Stirling (3), whither James had been taken soon after his birth, and entrusted to the care of the Earl of Mar. Whilst his coronation took place in the Church of the Holy Rood in the town, James himself was brought up in the castle.

Set high above the surrounding countryside, Stirling's strategic importance was appreciated for centuries – control of Stirling generally led to control of the country. From its windows, James would have been able to see the battlefield of Bannockburn, where Robert the Bruce had defeated Edward II of England, and the field of Sauchieburn where his great-great grandfather, James III, had been defeated, and replaced with James IV. It would also become the site of some personal distress as the location for the assassination of his grandfather, the Regent Lennox, and of his friend, the nephew of his guardian, the Earl of Mar.

Stirling is well worth visiting. In the care of Historic Environment Scotland, it is full of interest – in particular, the redecoration of the royal apartments to show how they looked during the time of James' grandparents, James V and Marie of Guise.

By the time James was fourteen, he was endeavouring to govern himself, but his reliance on his paternal cousin, Esmé Stuart, Duke of Lennox, led to grumblings amongst his nobles. The Ruthven family, under the leadership of the Earl of Gowrie, abducted the young King and held him captive at Ruthven Castle (4) on the outskirts of Perth.

Ruthven is now known as Huntingtower Castle. It is in the care of Historic Environment Scotland, and is open to visitors.

James escaped from the Ruthvens by calling a conference of his other nobles at St Andrew's in Fife (5). He proclaimed his majority, and agreed to forgive and forget the past, and act as a just King over all his people. St Andrew's was the seat of the Archbishop of St Andrew's, the Primate of Scotland. The Cathedral had been sacked by a Protestant mob in 1559 but was still an important royal burgh.

Today, St Andrew's is a famous university town, with the ruins of the Cathedral making an imposing backdrop to the city. It is also the location of the St Andrew's Royal and Ancient Golf Club, which still regulates the game.

Over the following years, James attempted to control the country, but there were frequent rebellions, feuds between nobles for both religious and political reasons, and attempts to abduct, or even assassinate the king. Following a particularly flagrant piece of disobedience by the Earl of Huntly, who had been one of James' closest friends, even the normally unwarlike James felt constrained to take military action. In 1588, he raised an army to march on Huntly's power base in Aberdeen (6).

Finally in command, James, now twenty-three, sought a wife. After much discussion, Anne, a Princess of Denmark, was selected, and following a proxy marriage, she set sail for her new home. Unfortunately, severe storms repeatedly drove her fleet back into port. James, desperate for news of his bride, retreated to Craigmillar Castle (7) on the outskirts of Edinburgh to await her arrival. Eventually, when word came that she had had to take refuge in Oslo, he set out to fetch her himself. Craigmillar is an excellent example of a late mediaeval Scottish castle – it was here that the Craigmillar Bond was signed – the bond agreed by Mary's lords that formed the backdrop to the murder of Darnley – possibly with Mary's knowledge.

Despite Huntly's apparent defeat and disgrace, he was soon back in favour, and before long involved in one of the most notorious assassinations of the age. He and the Earl of Moray (son-in-law of the Regent Moray) had been feuding for years. James, convinced that he could reconcile them (or possibly party to a plot) arranged for the two earls to meet at Donibristle (or Dunibirsle) castle (8), which was located in the lands disputed between the two Earls. Huntly set fire to the castle with his enemy inside. When Moray managed to escape, he was followed to the beach and killed by Huntly in person. The remains of the castle are now incorporated into the eighteenth century Dunibirsle House at Dalgety Bay. The property is in divided into residential flats.

By the end of the century, James had Scotland more-or-less pacified, and obedient to royal command. The relative state of peace and prosperity enabled him to leave Scotland in 1603 when he inherited the throne of England.

On receiving the news that he had been proclaimed king by Elizabeth's former Privy Councillors, James set out from Edinburgh on a slow and elaborate progress south, stopping frequently en route. One of his longest stops was at Worksop Manor (9), a sumptuous mansion owned by the Earl of Shrewsbury. The earl was nervous, as he had been the chief gaoler of James' mother, Mary, Queen of Scots, and his wife's granddaughter, Lady Arbella Stuart, was James' chief rival for the succession. Worksop was the first of the great Elizabethan Prodigy Houses that James saw, and he was amazed, and delighted, at the wealth, as he perceived it, of his new kingdom. The house was probably designed by Robert Smythson, who had worked on Longleat, and also Burghley.

No expense was spared by Shrewsbury, who sent out messages to all his neighbours, asking them to contribute provisions. There is a record in Ben Johnson's account of his trip through England in 1618, that during James' visit, part of the floor had fallen down in the Great Chamber (possibly meaning the upper floor, so the chamber's ceiling). However, the incident cannot have been particularly noteworthy, as there is no other known mention of it. In 1701 the house was renovated, but all trace of the Elizabethan house disappeared following a fire in 1767. The estate, which was sold several times, is in private hands.

When James eventually reached London, he would have seen St Paul's Cathedral (10). It was at St Paul's that the Privy Council would have had the Proclamation of his succession read out. The Cathedral was in a poor state of repair. In 1608, James urged the Bishop of London, Richard Bancroft, to repair it, but the church was impoverished following the Dissolution of the Monasteries which brought most of its former lands into private hands. Famously, St Paul's was utterly destroyed by the Great Fire of 1666. The current structure, designed by Sir Christopher Wren, was completed during the reign of James' great-granddaughter, Queen Anne.

James, like his predecessor, undertook several progresses, largely along the Thames Valley, to show himself to his subjects. This included visits to the city of Oxford (11) where James approved the foundation of Pembroke College in 1624. The College was named for James' courtier, Sir William Herbert, 3rd Earl of Pembroke. William's brother, Philip Herbert, 1st Earl of Montgomerie, was a great favourite of James, and their mother, Lady Mary Sidney, Countess of Pembroke, was another of his friends. The Countess was one of the most famous scholars of the whole Renaissance period, and one of the first women to achieve literary fame.

James visited the Pembrokes at Wilton House (12) in Salisbury, and the Countess arranged for The King's Men, including Shakespeare, to perform. Wilton, originally an Abbey, was granted to Sir William Herbert, 1st Earl of Pembroke, the brother-in-law of Queen Katherine Parr. He built the house that James would have known, but it was demolished in 1630, and the current house, still the home of the Earls of Pembroke, replaced it. Wilton is open to the public.

The Countess of Pembroke was granted lands in Bedfordshire by James, where she built the delightful hunting box, Houghton House (13). She entertained the King there in 1621.

Of all the mansions he saw in England, the one James most liked was Theobalds (14) in Hertfordshire. Built by Lord Burghley for his second son, Sir Robert Cecil, Elizabeth had frequently visited it, and James was equally enamoured. It was here that he first received the formal allegiance of Elizabeth's Privy Council, and here that he entertained his brother-in-law, Christian IV of Denmark, in 1606. In 1607, he persuaded Cecil to exchange it for Hatfield House. The house was demolished under Cromwell, and only a few traces remain. James died at Theobalds on 27th March 1625.

During his life-time, James had made some changes in the Henry VII chapel in Westminster Abbey (15), where he was to be buried. He moved the body of Elizabeth to the tomb of Mary I, brought his mother's remains from Peterborough Cathedral, and greatly enhanced the tomb of his grandmother, Lady Margaret Douglas, Countess of Lennox. He also commissioned elaborate tombs for his two daughters, Mary and Sophia, who died young. Prince Henry Frederick, although buried in the chapel has no monument – he shares a tomb with his sister, Elizabeth, Queen of Bohemia (grandmother of the eventual heir to the Stuarts, George of Hanover). James himself was buried in the vault of Henry VII and Elizabeth of York. Anne of Denmark is also buried in the chapel, but does not share her husband's grave.

The list below corresponds to the map which follows of places James VI & I would have known.

Key to Map

1. Holyrood Palace, Edinburgh, Scotland
2. Edinburgh castle, Edinburgh, Scotland
3. Stirling Castle, Stirling, Scotland
4. Ruthven Castle, Perth, Scotland
5. St Andrew's, Fife, Scotland
6. Aberdeen, Aberdeenshire, Scotland
7. Craigmillar Castle, Edinburgh, Scotland
8. Donibristle Castle, Fife, Scotland
9. Worksop Castle, Nottinghamshire, England
10. St Paul's Cathedral, London, England
11. Oxford, Oxfordshire, England
12. Wilton House, Salisbury, Wiltshire, England
13. Houghton House, Ampthill, Bedfordshire, England
14. Theobalds, Cheshunt, Hertfordshire, England
15. Westminster Abbey, London, England

Map

Chapter 25: King James Bible

The King James Authorised Version of the Bible is the best-selling text ever written in English. The elegance of its language, the majesty of its prose when read aloud, and the influence it has had on the culture of the English-speaking world is unrivalled.

But it has also been a political tool, both at the time of writing, and through the ages. In the four hundred years since it was first published it has been loved, hated, revered and reviled. Today, it tends to be heard on high-days and holidays: the generation born in the 1960s was probably the last to hear it as part of everyday life in school assemblies or in church. With few Anglicans attending church regularly, and the majority of services using the Revised English Bible of 1989, it is fading from our culture, but leaving aside religious belief, the King James Bible deserves to be appreciated as a magnificent work of literature.

The genesis of the idea sprang from the Hampton Court Conference convened by James VI & I in January 1604. Its purpose was to reconcile the Puritan wing of the Anglican Church to the mainstream.

The Anglican Church, in the Book of Common Prayer of 1552, as amended in 1559 and enforced by the Acts of Uniformity and Subscription, laid down rules about matters that were described as '*indifferent*', that is, there were no specific instructions in the Bible about them. The Church authorities wanted the rules about '*indifferent*' matters to be observed, so that there was uniformity of worship, considered to be vitally important. The Puritans, on the other hand, objected to indifferent matters that were not specifically in the Bible. James believed that he would be able to reconcile these conflicting views. With an immense belief in his own erudition, he thought that he would be able to convince the Puritans that they should follow the rules.

The major bones of contention were over ecclesiastical dress, the use of rings in wedding ceremonies, Confirmation, the presence of the crucifix and other matters that the Puritans believed were essentially Catholic practices, from which the Church ought to be purified.

In addition, there were concerns that the Sabbath was not properly observed, that the clergy were not sufficiently educated to teach their flocks and that pluralism (the holding of more than one position or 'benefices' in the Church) was rife. All these matters were to be addressed.

Most English Puritans, unlike the Presbyterians in Scotland, did not want to change the structure of the Church, although there was a hard core who did. The governance of the Church in England was '*Episcopalian*' that is, it was led by a hierarchy of bishops (*ebiscopus* in Latin, which is derived from Greek *episkopos*, which may also be translated as overseer).

Bishops had existed in the Church for centuries, and it was believed that they were the direct spiritual descendants of the Apostles. When a bishop was consecrated, he underwent the ceremony of '*laying on of hands*' – that is, other bishops laid their hands on him to transmit the link from the Apostles – '*Apostolic*

Succession'. In England, Apostolic Succession was unbroken, as the first Reformation Archbishop of Canterbury, Thomas Cranmer, had been instituted as a bishop in the traditional format, as had Matthew Parker, Elizabeth's first Archbishop.

Before the Reformation, Bishops were appointed by the Pope, usually on the basis of a recommendation by the monarch, or other influential figure. After the Reformation in England, bishops were appointed by the Crown. It was thus a system of control of the Church from the top.

The Presbyterians saw this as Catholic superstition and believed that the early Church was led by Ministers and Elders selected by the congregation, and that that should be emulated by contemporary Christians – it was an important tenet of their belief that Church members should approve those in authority, who would represent their congregations at *'Presbyteries'*. This organisation had been implemented in Scotland by the 1560 Confession of Faith, and by the First and Second Books of Discipline.

For monarchs, such ideas were a dangerous flirtation with democracy – in the sixteenth century considered the equivalent of mob-rule. For James, the strength of the Presbyterian movement in Scotland had been a thorn in his side – so far as the Scottish Kirk was concerned, he was no more important than any other member, and ought to be guided by the ministers, and the General Assembly. James proclaimed his view of Presbyterianism with the words *'it agreeth as well with monarchie as God and the devil.'*

At the Hampton Court Conference, James would deal only with the moderate Puritans, refusing to involve the '*brainsick and heady preachers*'.   Thus, the four divines representing the reformers, Dr Reynolds of President of Corpus Christi College, Oxford; Laurence Chaderton, Master of Emmanuel College, Cambridge; Thomas Sparks and John Knewstubs, were friends and colleagues of the Archbishop, John Whitgift and his eight bishops.   All of those involved were Protestant, in that they rejected the doctrine of transubstantiation, and embraced the principle of justification by faith alone.   No Catholics were invited to attend, as, according to the law, all Catholic priests had been banished from England (with the minor exception of those ordained before the death of Mary I in 1558, 46 years before).

After heated and acrimonious debate, in which some points were agreed (mainly regarding pluralism and the need for an educated clergy – hardly contentious), Dr Reynolds opined that he wished there were '*one only translation of ye byble to be authenticall and read in ye churche*'

James seized on the idea with glee.   There were several English bibles in use in England and the most popular one, the Geneva, was heartily disapproved of by the king, because of its copious marginal notes, giving a Presbyterian gloss, and, most displeasingly of all, praising biblical acts of disobedience to royal authority, where to obey would be sinful.

The new translation (which was not to have any marginal notes at all) was to be undertaken by the most learned doctors of the two universities, reviewed by the bishops, approved by the Privy

Council, and to finally be subject to royal assent. Once it was approved by the king, no other translation could be used in public worship. Clearly, the new translation was going to be Episcopalian, and a firm upholder of royal authority. That is not to say that James wanted anything but an accurate, robust and credible translation, based on the very best scholarship.

Archbishop Whitgift died not long after the conference, to be replaced by Richard Bancroft. Bancroft had initially objected to the idea of a new translation, but once the king had decided on it, he wholeheartedly set to work to turn James' dream into reality. A flurry of instructions and orders poured from his pen, embodying James' vision in practical arrangements.

Unlike Tyndale's Bible, which had been the work of a single, inspired, individual, the new translation was to be created by a committee, as had been the Great Bible of 1539 and the Bishops' Bible of 1568. The latter had been translated, rather poorly, according to scholars of the time, by fourteen men, each responsible for three or four books. Similarly, the Douai Bible of 1582, created by the English Catholic exiles, was also a team effort. Such collaborative efforts were entirely consistent with other literary endeavour – many of Shakespeare and his contemporaries' plays were collaborations. Unlike committee authorship today, which so often produces turgid and impenetrable prose, educated Jacobeans had mastered the art of creating a whole from individual parts.

Originally, there were to be fifty-four Translators, divided into 'companies' of eight men, each headed by a director. They were to translate from the original Hebrew, Greek and Aramaic texts on the basis of fifteen specific rules, which may be summarised as follows:

1. The translation was to build, so far as was consistent with faithful translation, on the Bishops' Bible. In the event, this original was so far from perfect that it is estimated that it contributed less than 10% to the final product;

2. Names of biblical characters were to be rendered in the style most familiar to readers or listeners, for example '*Timothy*' was not translated as '*Fear-God*', which was the style the Puritans preferred, and which gave rise to derision as the more devout named their children '*Sorry-for-sin*', '*Fear-not*', '*Eschew-evil*' and the like.

3. Perhaps most contentiously for the Puritans, the Translators were to keep traditional renditions of certain words – church, not congregation; priest, not elder and so forth;

4. Where a word had several possible meanings, the meaning ascribed to it in previous translations was to be preferred, so long as it was correct;

5. Chapter divisions were to be retained, so far as possible;

6. Marginal notes were to be added only where a Greek or Hebrew word could not easily be translated into a simple English expression;

1. Where one verse quoted another verse, they were to be cross-referenced in the margin;

2. Within each company, individual Translators were to work separately on the same sections, then compare their work and agree a final version;

3. As each section was completed by a company, it was to be reviewed by the other companies;

4. If the reviewing company were unhappy with the original translation, they were to inform the translating company, and, at the end all the directors would review the contentious part and resolve the matter;

5. Where there was uncertainty, scholars not on the translation team could be consulted;

6. Each bishop was to ask for the opinion of his clergy;

7. The directors were named, and included Dr Reynolds and Dr Chaderton who had represented the Puritans at the Hampton Court Conference;

8. The translations, other than the Bishops' Bible, that could be consulted, were: Tyndale's, Matthew's; Coverdale's, Whitchurch's and the Geneva version;

9. Where the New Testament quotes the Old (frequently in the mouths of Jesus and the Apostles), a group of external scholars was to check that the quotes were consistent with the original verses.

The Reformation had left the English church poor, and it was immediately apparent that the Translators would need to have enough to live on whilst they were doing their work. The Bishops were asked to grant benefices sufficient to allow each Translator to have an annual stipend of £20 (about the level of income of a well-off yeoman or minor gentleman). Details do not survive of whether this was done.

There is no definitive record of how the Translators organised their work, although there are indications that some of the Companies had regular weekly meetings. A few documents have been found that were working papers, but no largescale drafts.

In spring 1611, the final product, reviewed by Bancroft, the Privy Council and the King, and with a preface, chapter heads and titles added by the Bishop of Gloucester, was sent to the printer, Richard Barker.

After all the work, the result was something of a damp squib. Barker, the King's Printer, made a mull of the printing. Pages were muddled, there were frequent mis-prints, the already-old-fashioned gothic typeface was confused with random words in italics, originally meant to indicate a word in Greek or Hebrew and the cross-referencing referred to the old Latin Vulgate bible. This disappointing state of affairs was compounded over the centuries (there was even a 1631 edition that rendered Exodus 1: 14 as 'Thou shalt commit adultery'). During the nineteenth century, there were reckoned to be some 24,000 variations between the extant copies.

Many people thought the language archaic and the Puritans disliked it. The Geneva Bible continued to be the most popular version, until further printing of it was forbidden in 1616, from which time the new bible became the only 'authorised' version, although there is no extant documentation relating to the relevant order. Geneva Bibles continued to be imported from foreign presses.

After the Restoration, the King James Bible began to be appreciated, perhaps in part as the symbol of that Utopia of 'before the war'. In the new states of America, the Geneva Bible also began to give place to the King James Bible. Over the following centuries, its place in the heart of English-speaking culture grew. Revisions were made in the late nineteenth century, but a wholesale new translation was not begun until after World War II, resulting in the New English Bible, which T S Eliot described as a book 'astonish(ing) in its combination of the vulgar, the trivial and the pedantic.'

It is hard to imagine that any work will stand the test of time better than the King James Bible – a work of prodigious scholarship, collaborative endeavour and literary brilliance.

Chapter 26: Book Review

There are few books about James VI, although interest in him is increasing and there is a general reassessment of him as a more effective king than he is often credited with being.   A recent biography is John Matusiak's *'James I: Scotland's King of England'*.   An interesting take on the transition period of 1603 – 4 is Leanda de Lisle's *'After Elizabeth: The death of Elizabeth and the coming of King James'*.

Author: Leanda de Lisle

Publisher: Harper Perennial

In a nutshell: A rich and complex investigation of a period that is usually skated over – the transition from the Tudor to the Stuart dynasty in England.

Ms de Lisle's skill lies in unearthing fascinating detail about little known topics, and this is as apparent in this, her earliest published work, as in her later work on the Grey sisters (*Sisters of Treason*) and the Tudor family (*Tudor: The Family Story*).

In *After Elizabeth* she examines the period of transition around the turn of the seventeenth century when James VI of Scotland became James I of England. Because, ultimately, James took control without major incident, we tend to assume that it was all plain sailing. De Lisle shows us what was going on behind the scenes: the uncertainty which had permeated all levels of society about the succession for over forty years; the nervous anticipation in an England that had endured nearly ten years of plague, famine and war and was hoping for change; the secret hopes of Catholics that they would be allowed to emerge from the shadows and worship in freedom after forty-five years of oppression; the vision of the Puritans who hoped for a cleansing of the church. Most of all, the eager anticipation of many of Elizabeth's courtiers for a new king whom they hoped would spread largesse in their direction.

James was not the only contender for the English throne, but it is clear that the Privy Council, dominated by Robert Cecil, favoured his candidacy, which was certainly the strongest hereditary claim. De Lisle traces the history of Cecil's courting of James who had once been in correspondence by Cecil's arch rival, the Earl of Essex. Having seen off Essex, who, whilst undoubtedly talented and charismatic, was his own worst enemy, Cecil planned a careful campaign to ensure that he would remain in position as the monarch's chief secretary of state. Cecil's careful positioning of himself, and his manipulation of the situation to leave his rivals, such as Sir Walter Raleigh, out in the cold are gracefully depicted.

We follow James on his progress through his new kingdom and learn some fascinating details about what was going on in the background – the Earl of Shrewsbury's pleas to his neighbours to send poultry for the royal table, and Lady Anne Clifford's observation that she and her mother had caught lice from one of James' entourage, Sir Thomas Erskine. Everywhere de Lisle picks up the clash of cultures between the English and Scottish courts which James, despite his best efforts, never really overcame.

With so much expectation, it was inevitable that James could not please everyone. De Lisle shows how anticipation turned to disappointment, in the short term expressed with a flurry of small plots – the Main Plot and the Bye Plot, presaging the Gunpowder Plot and the discontent of the Puritans, which would culminate forty-five years later in the Civil War.

As always, Ms de Lisle manages to convey enormous amounts of detail in an elegant and readable style.

Bibliography

2016,   *The   parliament   of   1614*   (1964)
http://www.historyofparliamentonline.org/volume/1604-
1629/survey/

de Lisle, Leanda, *After Elizabeth: The death of Elizabeth and the coming of king James* (United Kingdom: Harper Perennial, 2006)

History, *Hanover historical texts collection: History department: Hanover   college*   (2015),
http://history.hanover.edu/project.php#ma

Matusiak, John, *James I: Scotland's King of England*, Kindle edn ([n.p.]: The History Press, 2015)

Melville, James Sir, Gordon Donaldson, and Melville Sir James, *The memoirs of sir James Melville of Halhill, containing an impartial account of the most remarkable affairs of state during the sixteenth century not mentioned by other historians, more particularly relating to the kingdoms of England and Scotland under* (London: Folio Society, 1969)

Nichols, John, *The progresses, Processions, and magnificent festivities, of king James the First, his royal Consort, family, and court: Collected from original Mss., scarce pamphlets, corporation records, Parochials registers, &C., &C volume 1* (United States: Arkose Press, 2015)

Nicolson, Adam, *When God spoke English: The making of the King James Bible. By Adam Nicolson* (London: Harper Press, 2011)

Oliver, Neil, *A History of Scotland*, Kindle edn (London: Phoenix (an Imprint of The Orion Publishing Group Ltd), 2009)

Somerset, Anne, *Unnatural murder: Poison in the court of James I: The Overbury murder* (London: Phoenix (an Imprint of The Orion Publishing Group Ltd), 1998)

Stedall, Robert, *The Survival of the Crown Volume II: The Return to Authority of the Scottish Crown following Mary Queen of Scots' Deposition from the Throne 1567-1603*, Kindle edn ([n.p.]: Book Guild Publishing, 2014)

www.tudortimes.co.uk

Printed in Great Britain
by Amazon

60749564R00059